AMERICAN POETS PROJECT

IS PUBLISHED WITH A GIFT IN MEMORY OF

James Merrill

AND SUPPORT FROM ITS FOUNDING PATRONS

Sidney J. Weinberg, Jr. Foundation

The Berkley Foundation

Richard B. Fisher and Jeanne Donovan Fisher

Kenneth Koch

selected poems

ron padgett editor

AMERICAN POETS PROJECT

THE LIBRARY OF AMERICA

Introduction, volume compilation, and notes copyright © 2007 by Literary
Classics of the United States, Inc. All rights reserved. Printed in the United States
of America. No part of this book may be reproduced in any manner whatsoever
without permission.

Copyright © 1998 by Kenneth Koch and © 2005 by The Kenneth Koch Literary
Estate. Published by arrangement with Alfred A. Knopf, a division of Random
House, Inc.

The paper used in this publication meets the minimum requirements of the
American National Standard for Information Sciences—Permanence of Paper
for Printed Library Materials, ANSI Z39.48—1984.

Design by Chip Kidd and Mark Melnick.
Frontispiece: Chris Felver

Library of Congress Cataloging-in-Publication Data:
Koch, Kenneth, 1925–2002.
  [Poems. Selections]
  Selected poems / Kenneth Koch ; Ron Padgett, editor.
    p. cm. — (American poets project ; 24)
  Includes bibliographical references and index.
  ISBN-13: 978-1-59853-006-3 (alk. paper)
  ISBN-10: 1-59853-006-2 (alk. paper)
    I. Padgett, Ron, 1942– II. Title.

PS3521.O27A6 2007
811'.54 — dc22   2006048657

10 9 8 7 6 5 4 3 2 1

Kenneth
Koch

CONTENTS

INTRODUCTION

It is a happy coincidence that the first line of poetry in this book is an exclamation and the last poem begins with the idea of excitement, for throughout his life Kenneth Koch was highly energized by the mystery and pleasure of being alive and by writing poetry that became a part of that mystery and pleasure. The selection of poems in this volume tracks his excitement that began with rambunctious and inventive literary fireworks and deepened over the years into a moving lyricism that never lost its freshness, mirroring a life whose anxieties and doubts were transmuted into adventure and joy.

In retrospect, Koch's becoming a poet seems never to have been in doubt. Born in Cincinnati in 1925, Kenneth wrote, at the age of seven, his first poem—four rhymed lines he copied a few years later into a notebook that he called *Scribble-ins of Kenneth Koch*, a collection of his own writing and comic strips. His mother, proud of her precocious only child, sometimes had him stand on a chair and recite his poems—"my first fan," he later called her.

Lillian Loth Koch, a lover of high culture and beauty, was by nature theatrical. She studied famous women of history and then created monodramas about them, which she performed for women's clubs in and around Cincinnati. But in personal relationships the vibrant Lilly fluctuated unpredictably between charming and difficult. Kenneth's father, Stuart, was calm, stable, and gentlemanly, but something of a bystander in the family dynamics. An executive in the Loth family's furniture business, he provided a comfortable upper-middle-class life for his wife and son. Lilly's and Stuart's forebears were Austrian and German Jews, respectively, who had immigrated in the mid-nineteenth century to Cincinnati.

That Kenneth was bright, talented, and literary is evident in "Ballad Salad," a clever parody he wrote in ninth grade. The following excerpt describes a few of the activities of a "bonny bandit":

> All things was wrong was what he done
> He ne'er done nae thing neece
> He tuke awee Durante's nose
> And tuke an eskimo's eece[1]

Literary encouragement came to young Koch from several sources. When he was fifteen his uncle, Leo Loth, gave him a treasured copy of Shelley's poems and applauded his interest in poetry. Two years later, Louis Untermeyer's anthology *Modern American and British Poetry* introduced him to the work of E. E. Cummings, Kenneth Patchen, William Carlos Williams, Ezra Pound, and Louis MacNeice, who became immediate influences. He was also impressed by the stream-of-consciousness passages in John Dos Passos's novel *U.S.A.* When his own poems took an aggressively experimental turn ("Fully agrandusating the milliamterical convolutions of each ackrested")[2] or ex-

---

[1] New York Public Library, Berg collection, series I, box 1, folder 1.

[2] Unpublished "Fat Woman and Nun on a Bus in June," Koch archive, Berg Collection, series I, box 1, folder 5.

pressed "unacceptable" feelings (such as the pleasure of crushing a baby's head), his high school English teacher, Katherine Lappa, calmly continued to praise his writing. In his final semester at Walnut Hills High School, where he edited the school literary magazine, his poetic production speeded up, perhaps in anticipation of what was to come after graduation.

With America's entry into World War II it became clear that Koch would be drafted. During the spring semester of his senior year in high school (1943) he attended the University of Cincinnati in a course of study that he hoped would lead him into a relatively safe job (meteorology) in the military; but the young man "who had gone about for years as a child / Praying God don't let there ever be another war / Or if there is, don't let me be in it" ("To World War Two") eventually found himself in the 96th Division, Army Infantry, shipped off to fight in the Pacific. Private Koch maintained his subscription to *View*, the surrealist avant-garde art and literary magazine, but life itself became surreal. Gangling at six feet tall and 150 pounds, he fought from start to finish in the battle of Leyte, where, on one patrol in the jungle, he lost his glasses and at every sound of gunfire dropped to the ground and shot blindly into the air. At another point, standing in a foxhole at dawn, he learned that a nearby fellow soldier had had his throat slit during the night. But throughout the nightmare of war, Koch clung to a sense of his destiny, telling himself, "I can't be killed—because of my poetry. I have to live on in order to write it" ("To World War Two"), a grandiose vision he later found amusing. As luck would have it, he contracted hepatitis and was evacuated to a hospital on Guam just as his division entered one of the bloodiest engagements in U.S. military history—the battle of Okinawa, in which the 96th Division suffered very heavy casualties.

Two months after Koch's discharge in January 1946,

he entered Harvard. Although the college did not normally accept transfer students, his College Board verbal score of a perfect 800, his high recommendations, and his good interview with an admissions officer showed him to be exceptional. An undergraduate majoring in English, he was thrilled to study with a real poet, the only one he had ever met: Delmore Schwartz. When, at Schwartz's urging, he embarked on a close study of Wallace Stevens and W. B. Yeats, his own work took on some of the latter's mythic aura. Later he was to shed Yeats's influence, but he continued to regard him as a great poet. Koch's admiration for Stevens never diminished.

The list of Harvard and Radcliffe undergraduates at the time who later became nationally known poets is impressive: among them Robert Creeley, Donald Hall, Robert Bly, and Adrienne Rich. However, the most significant for Koch was John Ashbery. The two met in the fall of 1947 in the office of the Harvard *Advocate*, the literary magazine edited at that time by Koch, and became fast friends.

Although at Harvard Koch's work temporarily took a morose turn due to bouts of depression and anxiety, he never stopped writing poems and plays; and he continued the process, begun in the military, of learning how to get along with a wider variety of people than he had known in Cincinnati. His amorous experiences in the army had been fleeting ones with women he never saw again, whereas at Harvard he felt a genuine affection for some of his girlfriends. Nevertheless, he found it hard to trust fully the people he got close to, and he remained socially insecure, at times formal or aloof, partly because of his stammer, partly because he was a Jew in a school whose traditions had not been favorable to Semites.

Aided by credit for his studies at the University of Cincinnati and the Illinois Institute of Technology (the latter as part of his army training), Koch earned a B.A. degree in the spring of 1948. But what was next? His father had hoped that he would come into the furniture business, but that was out of the question. First the military and then college had allowed Kenneth to distance himself from Cincinnati, and he had no intention of returning to the flatness of bourgeois life there. One suspects that he also wanted to get away from his mother, whom he loved but who drove him to distraction. Where was a brilliant, ambitious young man to go but to New York City?

Koch spent the next several years there, doing graduate work at Columbia (1949–50) and keeping in touch with Ashbery, who wrote to Koch about the work of another Harvard undergraduate, Frank O'Hara: "I think we have a new contender." O'Hara subsequently became a lifelong friend. That at an early age Koch developed enduring literary friendships with Ashbery and O'Hara suggests either his prescience or resounding good taste or both.

During this period in New York, Koch met two young painters who would also become lasting friends, Jane Freilicher and Larry Rivers. Freilicher recalled that one day, just as the Third Avenue elevated subway train was going past the building where she and Koch had apartments, passengers were taken aback to see, in one window, a gorilla staring out at them—that is, Koch wearing a gorilla mask. His genius for the comic was starting to reemerge, but it hardly showed in his new work: formal and rather middling pieces (sonnets, canzones, and allegorical poems in rhymed couplets) that grew out of his admiration for W. H. Auden's technical expertise.

The summer of 1950 found Koch briefly in Cincinnati, trying to improve his French and being dazzled by the poetry of Guillaume Apollinaire, just before leaving for a year in Paris and Aix-en-Provence as a Fulbright fellow. Apollinaire's lyricism, supple syntax, and long lines offered

Koch exciting new ways to leap out of his own temporary stylistic muddle.

In Aix Koch fell for one of the great loves of his life—the French language—and for the modern poetry of Max Jacob (for its combination of humor and anxiety), Pierre Reverdy (for its spareness and quiet mysteriousness), Paul Eluard (for its serious, lyrical eroticism), and St.-John Perse (for its majestic expansiveness), as well as the work of André Breton, René Char, Francis Ponge, and Henri Michaux. But he loved classic French poetry as well. Paul Valéry's writings on poetry appealed to him; he would often quote Valéry's definition of poetry as something written by someone other than the author to someone other than the reader. That French was a language Koch sometimes misunderstood added to its allure: for him the surprises of misunderstanding generated a new excitement about the sensuous properties of language and its possibilities for associative leaps.

He returned to America eager to tell his New York friends about the wonders of Europe. After sharing a house with Rivers and Freilicher in East Hampton in the summer of 1953, Koch was off again, this time to Berkeley for graduate work at the University of California. There he fell in love with Mary Janice Elwood, an intelligent and beautiful young woman of Quaker background and a fellow student in English. He found himself also in love, for the first time, with Walt Whitman's *Leaves of Grass*. Whitman's expansive cataloguing of everyday American wonders was a vast permission: "After I read Whitman I felt I could write about anything . . . His lines seem to rise from the pages of a book like trumpet sounds from microscopic chips embedded there."[3]

[3] *The Art of Poetry*, University of Michigan Press, pp. 188–89.

The first poem in the current volume, "Sun Out," written in 1952, has a number of the hallmarks of Koch's poetry: the title alone radiates optimism, and the first line seems to be welcoming the variety of the world ("Bananas, piers, limericks"). When it continues "I am postures / Over there, I, are / The lakes of delectation" it resonates with Arthur Rimbaud's "I is another," but in the second stanza Koch is not only another, he is everything else too! The poem's broken syntax and displaced semantics convey a happy liberation—a year before, Koch had written that "unsyntactical / Beauty might leap up!" (in "On the Great Atlantic Rainway")—but he maintains a sense of form by having the lines be of roughly the same length and in two equal stanzas.

It is hard to pin down Koch's method of composition in "Sun Up," but it might have resembled that of earlier poems, in which he sometimes revised by replacing certain words solely by phonic association. For example, as he later demonstrated (in "Days and Nights"):

> Sweet are the uses of adversity
> Became Sweetheart cabooses of diversity
> And Sweet art cow papooses at the university
> And sea bar Calpurnia flower havens' re-noosed knees

Koch was not simply trying to keep the language fresh, he was also assuming that there is always another kind of truth—a poetic truth that can be experienced even when it cannot be understood—behind every statement, a truth that sometimes can be discovered by an associative procedure such as this. As with a good abstract painting, what you see is what you get: an interesting or mysterious or beautiful surface. In his work there is no need for the reader to puzzle over symbols or decipher a cryptic poetic code. Koch had no use for the allusive obscurity that was rampant in American poetry in the 1940s and 50s. At various times he preferred the sensuousness of Keats, the dark lyricism of Lorca, the energy of Mayakovsky, the daring of Stein, the exalted depth of Rilke.

A year at Berkeley, far from New York and his friends there, was all that Koch could bear, so he transferred back to Columbia. To be nearer to him, Janice Elwood transferred to Harvard, then moved to New York, where the two shared an apartment on Perry Street in Greenwich Village. It was there, in the spring of 1953, that Koch wrote *When the Sun Tries to Go On*, a relentlessly energetic and fizzy abstract poem of 2,400 lines partly inspired by his reading *War and Peace*, a book that made him want to include everything imaginable,[4] but perhaps also by Whitman's long breath and urge toward vastness ("I contain multitudes") and by the sprung rhythm and piling up of words in the work of Gerard Manley Hopkins ("Brute beauty and valour and act, oh, air, pride, plume, here"). Koch's poem begins with the supreme word of accumulation:

> And, with a shout, collecting coat hangers
> Dour rebus, conch, hip,
> Ham, the autumn day, oh how genuine!
> Literary frog, catch-all boxer, O
> Real! The magistrate, say "group," bower, undies
> Disk, poop, *Timon of Athens* . . .

Often during the three-month composition of this work Koch would talk on the phone with O'Hara, who was also writing a long poem (*Second Avenue*), and the two would read their day's work aloud to each other, in what proved to be a useful and friendly competition. Koch often commented on how helpful it was to be inspired by and

[4]See the endnotes in *Sun Out*, p. 142.

envious of the work of one's brilliant friends. In this respect he relied mostly on O'Hara, Ashbery, and later James Schuyler, as well as the painters Freilicher, Rivers, Fairfield Porter, and Alex Katz, though he was also energized by other artists he knew, such as Franz Kline and Willem de Kooning, and in subsequent decades by collaborating with Jim Dine, Red Grooms, Joe Brainard, Rory McEwen, Bertrand Dorny, and his daughter Katherine. Koch, O'Hara, Ashbery, and Schuyler even wrote collaborative works together. It was these four who would come to be called, for better or worse, the New York School of Poets.

It was also in 1953 that Koch completed his M.A. work with a thesis, *The Physician in English Drama*. This study was an outgrowth of his lifelong love of theater, but one suspects that it also derived from his fear of contagious diseases—one of his earliest memories was of painful shots necessitated by a typhoid epidemic—and from his psychoanalysis. In fact his thesis ends with a call for a new poetic drama in which the analyst will assume the traditional doctor's function of resurrector.

Sometime in the early 1950s Koch underwent intensive Freudian psychoanalysis (with Rudolf Loewinstein) to deal with his anxieties, his stammer, and what he felt to be the less attractive parts of his character—a therapy that proved beneficial. The wildly imaginative Koch must have taken quickly to the therapeutic technique of free-association.

By the end of his first stint of teaching at Rutgers (1953–54), the syntax in his poetry had reassembled itself, as in "I am crazier than shirttails / In the wind, when you're near" ("To You"), and he was writing the poems that would figure in his first major collection.

In 1954 Kenneth and Janice were married, and using an inheritance from his Uncle Leo, they went to Europe. A year later, after their daughter Katherine was born in

Rome, the family returned to New York and Koch took up teaching again at Rutgers. In 1957 Janice's Fulbright took them to Florence. There Koch wrote not his doctoral thesis, as he was supposed to, but his first epic narrative poem, *Ko, or a Season on Earth*, which features, among others, a Japanese pitcher whose fastball has so much velocity it can knock down a grandstand. Written in ottava rima and iambic pentameter—a rhythm Koch had practiced by using it for his notes in a course at Harvard and later by learning to speak in it—this comic extravaganza was inspired by Byron's witty and digressive *Don Juan* and Ariosto's dashing and digressive *Orlando Furioso*.

Everyday life, though, became scary when Janice miscarried and nearly died. The Kochs hastened back to America, where Kenneth resumed teaching, at Rutgers and at Brooklyn College, while completing his Ph.D. work at Columbia, a dissertation entitled *The Reception and Influence of American Poetry in France, 1918–1950*. In 1959 he joined the English and Comparative Literature department at Columbia, and, in his 43 subsequent years there, proved to be an inspiring teacher known for his spontaneous wit, good taste, high standards, and infectious love of great literature and art, for which he received the Harbison Award for Distinguished Teaching (1970). A surprising number of his students went on to become writers. He also directed the influential poetry workshop program at the New School (1958–66), creating a hotbed of the so-called Second Generation of the New York School of Poets.

In 1962 Grove Press brought out Koch's first big collection, *Thank You and Other Poems*, part of which had been written as early as 1951. Compared with *When the Sun Tries to Go On*, its syntax is conventional, but the energy, imagination, and lyricism are as lively as ever, ranging from love poems:

I love you as a sheriff searches for a walnut
That will solve a murder case unsolved for years
Because the murderer left it in the snow beside a window
Through which he saw her head, connecting with
Her shoulders by a neck, and laid a red
Roof in her heart. . . .

("To You")

to faux naïveté and parody (of William Carlos Williams's "This Is Just to Say"):

I chopped down the house that you had been saving to
live in next summer.
I am sorry, but it was morning, and I had nothing to do
and its wooden beams were so inviting.

("Variations on a Theme
by William Carlos Williams")

to a diatribe against the stuffy poetry of the 1950s:

"Oh to be seventeen years old
Once again," sang the red-haired man, "and not know
that poetry
Is ruled with the sceptre of the dumb, the deaf, and the
creepy!"

("Fresh Air")

to the flatness of conventional narrative:

As I was walking home just now, from seeing
Margaret and Norris off . . .

("The Departure from Hydra")

to a formal poem consisting mainly of rhymed sonnets ("The Railway Stationery"), a Disneyesque fantasia ("The Circus"), a comic list poem ("Taking a Walk with You"), and an ode to lunch ("Lunch"). The wide range of work in

Thank You suggests that Koch, always open to new possibilities, would not be confined to a single style, unless it be a very capacious one. Five of the poems in this debut collection—"To You," "Fresh Air," "Permanently," "Variations on a Theme by William Carlos Williams," and "You Were Wearing"—continue to be widely anthologized.

Koch's buoyancy became more grounded in the spring of 1968, during protests at Columbia by students angry about the Vietnam War and by some of the university's policies. In one incident he and other faculty linked arms to defend students from the oncoming police, and he was appalled when, in the ensuing fracas, an officer inflicted a cut on the head of F. W. Dupee, the distinguished older professor who had become Koch's academic mentor and father figure. Though Koch was never a political activist, he had always been quick to support an immediate good cause or to help a needy friend. Galvanized by the student protests and the awfulness of the war (and no doubt by his own wartime experiences and by Janice's Quaker pacifism), he wrote his first overtly political poem, but instead of writing against the war, which he said others could do better, he wrote "The Pleasures of Peace," which ends in a lyrical upsurge of optimism:

> And the big boats come sailing into the harbor for
>   peace
> And the little apes are running around the jungle for
>   peace
> And the day (that is, the star of day, the sun) is
>   shining for peace
> Somewhere a moustachioed student is puzzling over
>   the works of Raymond Roussel for peace
> And the Mediterranean peach trees are fast asleep for
>   peace

With their pink arms akimbo and the blue plums of
      Switzerland for peace

[. . .]

And the Alps, Mount Vesuvius, all the really big
      important mountains

Are rising for peace, and they're filled with rocks—
      surely it won't be long;

And Leonardo da Vinci's *Last Supper* is moving across
      the monastery wall

A few micrometers for peace, and Paolo Uccello's red
      horses

Are turning a little redder for peace, and the Anglo-
      Saxon dining hall

Begins glowing like crazy, and Beowulf, Robert E.
      Lee, Sir Barbarossa, and Baron Jeep

Are sleeping on the railways for peace and darting
      around the harbor

And leaping into the sailboats and the sailboats will
      go on

[. . .]

It will all be going on in connection with you, peace,
      and my poem, like a Cadillac of wampum

Unredeemed and flying madly, will go exploding
      through

New cities sweet inflated, planispheres, ingenious
      hair, a camera smashing

Badinage, cerebral stands of atmospheres, unequaled,
      dreamed of

Empeacements, candled piers, fumisteries, emphatic
      moods, terrestrialism's

Crackle, love's flat, sun's sweets, oh Peace, to you.

This climactic incantation is a good example of the
masterful variations on the list technique that Koch used in

many of his best poems, topped off here with the stunning description of the poem itself as a flying "Cadillac of wampum." One wonders if he might have had Allen Ginsberg in mind, if obliquely, when he created in this poem a rival peace poet named Giorgio Finogle. Both Ginsberg and Koch were literary descendants of Whitman and Williams, and as different as Allen and Kenneth were, their work has remarkable similarities: spontaneity, high energy, expansiveness, a yearning for joy, the feeling that poetry can change the world. These qualities enabled them to invent hilarious collaborative poems before a live audience at the Poetry Project in 1979, documented in their book *Making It Up*.

In 1968 Koch started teaching poetry writing to children in a public elementary school on New York's Lower East Side. In doing so he started a quiet and happy revolution in how teachers think of their students and how students think of themselves, simply by honoring the energy of the imagination liberated by language. When he walked into the classroom, the children would cheer. Soon poets all over the country, inspired by Koch, were introducing schoolchildren to the joyous liberation of imaginative writing and thinking. Koch's trailblazing work is documented in his best-selling books *Wishes, Lies, and Dreams* (1970) and *Rose, Where Did You Get That Red?* (1973). For a while his national renown as a teacher overshadowed that of his own poetry, much to his dismay. Later he taught poetry writing to children in France, Italy, Haiti, Malaysia, and China, as well as to residents in a nursing home.

To depict Kenneth Koch solely as a sparklingly imaginative poet of optimism is to ignore the undercurrent of anxiety that caused him to undergo psychoanalysis for most of the 1960s. He wrote explicitly about this undercurrent in poems such as "Alive for an Instant":

[. . .] I think I have three souls
One for love one for poetry and one for acting out
    my insane self
Not insane but boring but perpendicular but untrue
    but true
The three rarely sing together [. . .]
I eat the bacon I went down the slide I have a thun-
    derstorm in my inside I will never hate you
But how can this maelstrom be appealing? do you like
    menageries? my god
Most people want a man!

The poem ends with a scary image, rare in Koch: "I have a wild rat in my secrets from you."

Having a secure position as a professor—a job he grew to love and perhaps the only one suitable for him—helped stabilize his life and influenced his writing. During the early 1970s Koch's poetry took an instructional turn: "The Art of Love" is a take-off on Ovid in the form of a comic handbook written by a logical but deranged man (whose sexism some readers found offensive); "Some General Instructions" is a curious mixture of ironic and straightforward advice; and "The Art of Poetry" is a completely serious general guide and, perhaps not incidentally, a manual for understanding Koch's own poetry.

From this point onward Koch would write other poems about writing poetry, clarifying how writing and life have a synergistic effect that helps each to be more pleasurable, honest, mysterious, beautiful, and deeply experienced.

In the early 1970s Koch's poetry began to engage his demons more explicitly. After his separation (amicable) from Janice in 1971, he wrote one of his most moving autobiographical poems, "The Circus" (sometimes referred to as "The Circus" [II] to distinguish it from his earlier poem of the same name). As if written late at night, the new "Circus" is imbued with regret for the lost past, the memory of old friendships, and the oddness of looking back at one's previous selves. Recollecting also makes him realize

> . . . I was interested in my career
> And still am but now it is like a town I don't want to
> leave
> Not a tower I am climbing opposed by ferocious
> enemies

The enemies he refers to were perhaps some who recognized themselves as among those he had thumbed his nose at in "Fresh Air," and who now declined to review his work, belittled it, or gave it grudging praise. In the dominant atmosphere of the somewhat depressed and solemn academic poetry of the 1950s and 60s Koch had been, after all, a disarming rarity: a highly sophisticated and serious comic poet. But it was also his stylistic difference that led some to underestimate his work, for in many quarters the dominant aesthetic still called for a poetry that was tightly compressed ("jewel-like") or that displayed a measured, controlled artifice (the "well-wrought" poem), whereas Koch's work was constantly opening out and flexing its spirit. He once told me that although the conventional idea of revision—tightening, condensing, honing—has its obvious uses, it alone is too narrow; sometimes a draft could be improved by expanding the poem to twice its length.

Koch's turn toward autobiography continued in *The Burning Mystery of Anna in 1951* (1979), which contains direct and open poems such as "The Problem of Anxiety" and an account of an intense love affair, "To Marina." This volume also includes one of his most admired poems, "The Boiling Water," whose first line—"A serious moment for the water is when it boils"—signals that this poem may have a muted comic undertone but that Koch is aiming for something else by focusing soberly on a single moment and exploring its ramifications.

Finally, in 1980, he and Janice divorced (again, amicably), and when she fell ill and died the following year, it was a terrible loss for him, for the love and admiration he felt for her was real. He would continue to write about her for the rest of his life, even though he would be involved with other intelligent and attractive women. Koch could not live without women, recurring muses at the erotic heart of his inspiration, like the beautiful young art student in his poem "Fresh Air."

Over the years Koch had provided virtual guides to his own work, from "Fresh Air" to "The Art of Poetry," but in *Days and Nights* (1982) the title piece is about not only his own poetry but also its relation to his life:

> Wondering how much life and how much writing
>   there should be—
> For me, have the two become mostly the same?
> Mostly! Thank God for the mostly! Last night with
>   you
> I felt by that shaken and uplifted
> In a way that no writing could ever do.
> The body after all is a mountain and the words are a
>   mist—
> I love the mist. Heaven help me, I also love you.

But Koch needed poetry: "It helps me to be writing it helps me to breathe" and his youthful belief that "poetry was everything" had a way of not disappearing. The year after Janice's death Koch went on a reading and lecture tour of Africa, sponsored by the United States Information Agency. In an unpublished travel journal, he describes his daily activities, the sights and sounds, but he also lays his heart bare:

> And I wonder who on earth I am writing for anyway? [. . .] I am already "a poet." How much interest do I have really, as I head for non-being, in finding out—or in communicating—some truth? Since I feel sure the truth won't save me from extinction.[5]

But later in the journal, when his spirits have brightened, his comment on a line of poetry he had read shows that he is as fascinated as ever by language itself:

> As for the appeal of the line "O la danseuse Zannie Amaya de Bangui!" it's that the words, the physical words, are so much stronger than the "meaning," so that the line escapes from its parents' intentions for itself and becomes a free entity—for a while, at least, it really lives.

Although Koch never stopped loving words that had sparkling surfaces, his poetry was becoming less efferverscent and more introspective: "What's here if I'm not that same sensual Kenneth / Of years ago, nuts for exhilaration" and "Did you too ever feel it, like a promise / That there could be a perfect lifetime, Janice?" His answer: "I don't know" and "Nothing has come of this except my wonder / What it's about, before I'm shoveled under" ("Seasons on Earth"). He was sixty.

When Karen Culler, a pianist and education consultant Koch had met in 1977, moved in with him in 1989, a sort of relaxation came over him. They married five years later, and until he died (July 6, 2002) Karen was to remain

[5]Koch archive, Berg Collection, notebook in series XIII, box 244.

his wife, friend, astute fan, and energetic traveling companion on trips to Europe, Africa, Asia, South America, and Antarctica.

Koch's next collection, *One Train* (1994), begins with the poem "One Train May Hide Another," inspired by a railroad crossing sign he had seen in Africa. This poem is a synthesis of many of his gifts: a lyrical marriage of humor and seriousness in the form of an instructional list focused on one motif deftly varied. Also in this volume is "A Time Zone," in which Koch takes off from Apollinaire's poem "Zone," whose conversational tone and limber, sometimes enjambed lines are given shape by being subtly rhymed couplets. Koch travels back through time zones to his early years in New York City, and now, when he talks about his old friends, it is with the certainty that most readers will recognize their names, for his friends have become part of America's literary and artistic history, as he has. But Koch is not name-dropping, and what he says in "Currency," a poem about his early experiences in France, rings true here as well:

> I don't care about fame
> I have never cared about it I just want to be delighted
>   and I'm envious
> I want to be part of that enormous cake over there

At this point in his career he can call upon any side of his poetic genius, moving from direct statements about his character to narrative to an imaginative lyricism that is unsurpassed in twentieth-century American poetry, even in such a simple line as "The pink and yellow lines come marching down the boulevard Montparnasse."

Ever alert to new ways of writing or to new ways of seeing older forms of writing, Koch revitalized the apostrophe, or, as he once wittily defined it, "a poem in which you talk to someone or something that can't talk back."[6] At the age of fifteen Koch had been exhilarated by Shelley's talking to the West wind, and he himself had used apostrophes in poems; he had even had schoolchildren write apostrophes inspired by Blake's "Tyger." But he himself had never written a whole poem as an apostrophe. His *New Addresses* (2000), composed entirely of such poems, turned out to be perhaps his most accessible and popular collection. Imagine writing a poem in which you talk, as he did, to the word *yes*, or to World War II, or to orgasms. As he commented in *Making Your Own Days: The Pleasures of Reading and Writing Poetry*, talking to something mysterious or huge makes us feel less at a loss, as perhaps it did for John Donne when he wrote "Death, be not proud." Feeling more powerful and in control seems to have allowed Koch to write about an even wider range of his experience, and to do so with honesty, wit, perception, and freshness. In "To Jewishness" he finally speaks at length of his ethnicity, and with good humor, as in "How / Like a Bible with shoulders / Rabbi Seligmann is!"

In a journal kept during a trip to China in 1991, Kenneth had written:

> I . . . decided . . . that I wasn't going to think about death, cancer, old age, failing powers anymore (as little as possible) but just keep thinking about things that open up.[7]

Koch had survived two different kinds of cancer, and, despite the expected bad patches, his underlying attitude

[6]An impromptu remark at his *New Addresses* reading at the St. Mark's Poetry Project, if memory serves.

[7]Koch archive, Berg Collection, series XIII, box 245.

throughout had been surprisingly buoyant, especially for one who flinched at a sneeze. Vitality radiated from this man who, well into his seventies, would write every morning for three or four hours and then go bounding about the tennis court with high energy. As for old age, he admitted to fearing it, but, after all, he had to accept it: he ends his poem "To Old Age" simply with "Old age, here we are!" But notice that it concludes with an exclamation mark.

For decades Koch had been idolized by young poets, especially in New York, but in his later years critical esteem for his work finally came to the fore, with public praise from writers such as Frank Kermode, John Gardner, Thomas M. Disch, James Salter, David Lehman, Reed Whittemore, Stephen Spender, Aram Saroyan, Robert Coles, John Hollander, Gary Lenhart, Ken Tucker, John Ashbery, Jonathan Lethem, and Charles Simic. Volumes of his poetry appeared in French, German, Italian, Portuguese, Greek, Swedish, and Danish translation. Koch was elected to the American Academy of Arts and Letters and won the Bollingen Prize, the Bobbitt Library of Congress Prize, the Shelley Award for Poetry, and the Phi Beta Kappa Award for Poetry. He was also a finalist for the National Book Award and the Pulitzer Prize. The French government made him a Knight in the Order of Arts and Letters. Koch liked getting prizes and awards but he never confused them with greatness. A competitive man with high standards, he continued to vie happily with his literary heroes past and present.

Koch's final collection, some of which was written with the knowledge that he would probably not survive his third cancer, shows that his poetry continued to unfold. *A Possible World*, published a few months after his death, has much of his witty charm, but it also charts new directions in his work. One such direction is toward what I think deserves to be called profundity. Koch had always warned against solemnity, a trait often mistaken for seriousness, but at this point in his life his spirit seemed to move beyond seriousness, even. At least that is what I sense in "Paradiso," a poem whose title probably refers to Dante's heaven and whose final lines ask a question that most of us are unable to answer:

> . . . . . Why do you keep believing in this
> Reality so dependent on the time allowed it
> That it has less to do with your exile from the age you
>   are
> Than from everything else life promised that you
>   could do?

Kenneth Koch kept believing in this reality. Near the end of June 2002, his illness demanded a return to the hospital, but he held off to attend one last performance of his short plays. Helped onstage as the cast were taking their bows, he shuffled over to the director, smiled, and, with a courtly bow, offered her a rose.

Ron Padgett
2006

Sun Out

Bananas, piers, limericks
I am postures
Over there, I, are
The lakes of delectation
Sea, sea you! Mars and win-
Some buffalo
They thinly raft the plain,
Common do

It ice-floes, hit-and-run drivers,
The mass of the wind.
Is that snow
H-ing at the door? And we
Come in the buckle, a
Vanquished distinguished
Secret festival, relieving flights
Of the black brave ocean.

To You

I love you as a sheriff searches for a walnut
That will solve a murder case unsolved for years
Because the murderer left it in the snow beside a
        window
Through which he saw her head, connecting with
Her shoulders by a neck, and laid a red
Roof in her heart. For this we live a thousand years;
For this we love, and we live because we love, we are not

Inside a bottle, thank goodness! I love you as a
Kid searches for a goat; I am crazier than shirttails
In the wind, when you're near, a wind that blows from
The big blue sea, so shiny so deep and so unlike us;
I think I am bicycling across an Africa of green and
        white fields
Always, to be near you, even in my heart
When I'm awake, which swims, and also I believe that
        you
Are trustworthy as the sidewalk which leads me to
The place where I again think of you, a new
Harmony of thoughts! I love you as the sunlight leads
        the prow
Of a ship which sails
From Hartford to Miami, and I love you
Best at dawn, when even before I am awake the sun
Receives me in the questions which you always pose.

The Circus

I

We will have to go away, said the girls in the circus
And never come back any more. There is not enough of
        an audience
In this little town. Waiting against the black, blue sky
The big circus chariots took them into their entrances.
The light rang out over the hill where the circus wagons
        dimmed away.
Underneath their dresses the circus girls were sweating,
But then, an orange tight sticking to her, one spoke with

Blue eyes, she was young and pretty, blonde
With bright eyes, and she spoke with her mouth open
     when she sneezed.
Lightly against the backs of the other girls waiting in line
To clock the rope, or come spinning down with her
     teeth on the line,
And she said that the circus might leave—and red
     posters
Stuck to the outside of the wagon, it was beginning to
Rain—she said might leave but not her heart would ever
     leave
Not that town but just any one where they had been,
     risking their lives,
And that each place they were should be celebrated by
     blue rosemary
In a patch, in the town. But they laughed and said
     Sentimental
Blonde, and she laughed, and they all, circus girls, clinging
To each other as the circus wagons rushed through the
     night.

2

In the next wagon, the one forward of theirs, the next
     wagon
Was the elephants' wagon. A grey trunk dragged on the
     floor . . .

3

Orville the Midget tramped up and down. Paul the
     Separated Man
Leaped forward. It rained and rained. Some people in
     the cities

Where they passed through were sitting behind thick
    glass
Windows, talking about their brats and drinking
    chocolate syrup.

4

Minnie the Rabbit fingered her machine gun.
The bright day was golden.
She aimed the immense pine needle at the foxes
Thinking Now they will never hurt my tribe any more.

5

The circus wagons stopped during the night
For eighteen minutes in a little town called Rosebud,
    Nebraska.
It was after dinner it was after bedtime it was after
    nausea it was
After lunchroom. The girls came out and touched each
    other and had fun
And just had time to get a breath of the fresh air of the
    night in
Before the ungodly procession began once more down
    the purple highway.

6

With what pomp and ceremony the circus arrived
    orange and red in the dawn!
It was exhausted, cars and wagons, and it lay down and
    leaped
Forward a little bit, like a fox. Minnie the Rabbit shot a
    little woolen bullet at it,

And just then the elephant man came to his doorway in
    the sunlight and stood still.

7

The snoring circus master wakes up, he takes it on
    himself to arrange the circus.
Soon the big tent floats high. Birds sing on the tent.
The parade girls and the living statue girls and the
    trapeze girls
Cover their sweet young bodies with phosphorescent
    paint.
Some of the circus girls are older women, but each is
    beautiful.
They stand, waiting for their cues, at the doorway of the
    tent.
The sky-blue lion tamer comes in, and the red giraffe
    manager.
They are very brave and wistful, and they look at the
    girls.
Some of the circus girls feel a hot sweet longing in their
    bodies.
But now is it time for the elephants!
Slowly the giant beasts march in. Some of their legs are
    clothed in blue papier-mâché ruffles.
One has a red eye. The elephant man is at the peak of
    happiness.
He speaks, giddily, to every one of the circus people he
    passes,
He does not know what he is saying, he does not care—
His elephants are on display! They walk into the sandy
    ring . . .

8

Suddenly a great scream breaks out in the circus tent!

It is Aileen the trapeze artist, she has fallen into the dust
and dirt

From so high! She must be dead! The stretcher bearers
rush out,

They see her lovely human form clothed in red and
white and orange wiry net,

And they see that she does not breathe any more.

The circus doctor leaves his tent, he runs out to care for
Aileen.

He traverses the circus grounds and the dusty floor of
the circus entrance, and he comes

Where she is, now she has begun to move again, she is
not dead,

But the doctor tells her he does not know if she will ever
be able to perform on the trapeze again,

And he sees the beautiful orange and red and white form
shaken with sobs,

And he puts his hand on her forehead and tells her she
must lie still.

9

The circus girls form a cortege, they stand in file in the
yellow and white sunlight.

"What is death in the circus? That depends on if it is
spring.

Then, if elephants are there, *mon père*, we are not
completely lost.

Oh the sweet strong odor of beasts which laughs at decay!

Decay! decay! We are like the elements in a kaleidoscope,

But such passions we feel! bigger than beaches and
Rustier than harpoons." After his speech the circus
    practitioner sat down.

10

Minnie the Rabbit felt the blood leaving her little body
As she lay in the snow, orange and red and white,
A beautiful design. The dog laughs, his tongue hangs
    out, he looks at the sky.
It is white. The master comes. He laughs. He picks up
    Minnie the Rabbit
And ties her to a pine tree bough, and leaves.

11

Soon through the forest came the impassioned bumble
    bee.
He saw the white form on the bough. "Like rosebuds
    when you are thirteen," said Elmer.
Iris noticed that he didn't have any cap on.
"You must be polite when mother comes," she said.
The sky began to get grey, then the snow came.
The two tots pressed together. Elmer opened his mouth
    and let the snow fall in it. Iris felt warm and happy.

12

Bang! went the flyswatter. Mr. Watkins, the circus
    manager, looked around the room.
"Damn it, damn these flies!" he said. Mr. Loftus, the
    circus clerk, stared at the fly interior he had just
    exposed.

The circus doctor stood beside the lake. In his hand he
  had a black briefcase.
A wind ruffled the surface of the lake and slightly rocked
  the boats.

Red and green fish swam beneath the surface of the water.
The doctor went into the lunchroom and sat down. No,
  he said, he didn't care for anything to eat.
The soft wind of summer blew in the light green trees.

Permanently

One day the Nouns were clustered in the street.
An Adjective walked by, with her dark beauty.
The Nouns were struck, moved, changed.
The next day a Verb drove up, and created the Sentence.

Each Sentence says one thing—for example, "Although
  it was a dark rainy day when the Adjective walked
  by, I shall remember the pure and sweet expression
  on her face until the day I perish from the green,
  effective earth."
Or, "Will you please close the window, Andrew?"
Or, for example, "Thank you, the pink pot of flowers on
  the window sill has changed color recently to a light
  yellow, due to the heat from the boiler factory
  which exists nearby."

In the springtime the Sentences and the Nouns lay
   silently on the grass.
A lonely Conjunction here and there would call, "And!
   But!"
But the Adjective did not emerge.

As the adjective is lost in the sentence,
So I am lost in your eyes, ears, nose, and throat—
You have enchanted me with a single kiss
Which can never be undone
Until the destruction of language.

You Were Wearing

You were wearing your Edgar Allan Poe printed cotton
   blouse.
In each divided up square of the blouse was a picture of
   Edgar Allan Poe.
Your hair was blonde and you were cute. You asked me,
   "Do most boys think that most girls are bad?"
I smelled the mould of your seaside resort hotel
   bedroom on your hair held in place by a John
   Greenleaf Whittier clip.
"No," I said, "it's girls who think that boys are bad."
   Then we read *Snowbound* together
And ran around in an attic, so that a little of the blue
   enamel was scraped off my George Washington,
   Father of His Country, shoes.

Mother was walking in the living room, her Strauss
     Waltzes comb in her hair.

We waited for a time and then joined her, only to be
     served tea in cups painted with pictures of Herman
     Melville

As well as with illustrations from his book *Moby Dick* and
     from his novella *Benito Cereno.*

Father came in wearing his Dick Tracy necktie: "How
     about a drink, everyone?"

I said, "Let's go outside a while." Then we went onto the
     porch and sat on the Abraham Lincoln swing.

You sat on the eyes, mouth, and beard part, and 1 sat on
     the knees.

In the yard across the street we saw a snowman holding
     a garbage can lid smashed into a likeness of the mad
     English king, George the Third.

Variations on a Theme
by William Carlos Williams

1

I chopped down the house that you had been saving to
     live in next summer.
I am sorry, but it was morning, and I had nothing to do
and its wooden beams were so inviting.

2

We laughed at the hollyhocks together
and then I sprayed them with lye.
Forgive me. I simply do not know what I am doing.

3

I gave away the money that you had been saving to live
      on for the next ten years.
The man who asked for it was shabby
and the firm March wind on the porch was so juicy and
      cold.

4

Last evening we went dancing and I broke your leg.
Forgive me. I was clumsy, and
I wanted you here in the wards, where I am the doctor!

The Railway Stationery

The railway stationery lay upon
The desk of the railway clerk, from where he could see
The springtime and the tracks. Engraved upon
Each page was an inch-and-a-half-high T
And after that an H and then an E
And then, slightly below it to the right,
There was COLUMBUS RAILWAY COMPANY
In darker ink as the above was light.
The print was blue. And just beneath it all
There was an etching—not in blue, but black—
Of a real railway engine half-an-inch tall
Which, if you turned the paper on its back,
You could see showing through, as if it ran
To one edge of the sheet then back again.

To one edge of the sheet then back again!
The springtime comes while we're still drenched in snow
And, whistling now, snow-spotted Number Ten
Comes up the track and stops, and we must go
Outside to get its cargo, with our hands
Cold as the steel they touch. Inside once more
Once we have shut the splintery wooden door
Of the railway shack, the stationery demands
Some further notice. For the first time the light,
Reflected from the snow by the bright spring sun,
Shows that the engine wheel upon the right
Is slightly darker than the left-side one
And slightly lighter than the one in the center,
Which may have been an error of the printer.

Shuffling through many sheets of it to establish
Whether this difference is consistent will
Prove that it is not. Probably over-lavish
At the beginning with the ink, he still
(The printer) had the presence of mind to change
His operating process when he noticed
That on the wheels the ink had come out strange.
Because the windows of the shack are latticed
The light that falls upon the stationery
Is often interrupted by straight lines
Which shade the etching. Now the words "Dear Mary"
Appear below the engine on one sheet
Followed by a number of other conventional signs,
Among which are "our love," "one kiss," and "sweet."

The clerk then signs his name—his name is Johnson,
But all he signs is Bill, with a large B
Which overflows its boundaries like a Ronson
With too much fluid in it, which you see
Often, and it can burn you, though the *i*
Was very small and had a tiny dot.
The *l*'s were different—the first was high,
The second fairly low. And there was a spot
Of ink at the end of the signature which served
To emphasize that the letter was complete.
On the whole, one could say his writing swerved
More than the average, although it was neat.
He'd used a blue-black ink, a standing pen,
Which now he stuck back in its stand again.

Smiling and sighing, he opened up a drawer
And took an envelope out, which then he sealed
After he'd read the letter three times more
And folded it and put it in. A field
Covered with snow, untouched by man, is what
The envelope resembled, till he placed
A square with perforated edges that
Pictured a white-haired President, who faced
The viewer, in its corner, where it stuck
After he'd kissed its back and held it hard
Against the envelope. Now came the truck
Of the postman "Hello, Jim." "Hello there, Bill."
"I've got this—can you take it?" "Sure, I will!"

Now the snow fell down gently from the sky.
Strange wonder—snow in spring! Bill walked into
The shack again and wrote the letter *I*
Idly upon a sheet of paper. New
Ideas for writing Mary filled his mind,
But he resisted—there was work to do.
For in the distance he could hear the grind
Of the Seventy-Eight, whose engine was half blue;
So, putting on a cap, he went outside
On the tracks side, to wait for it to come.
It was the Seventy-Eight which now supplied
The city with most of its produce, although some
Came in by truck and some was grown in town.
Now it screams closer, and he flags it down.

Fresh Air

I

At the Poem Society a black-haired man stands up to say
"You make me sick with all your talk about restraint and
        mature talent!
Haven't you ever looked out the window at a painting by
        Matisse,
Or did you always stay in hotels where there were too
        many spiders crawling on your visages?
Did you ever glance inside a bottle of sparkling pop,
Or see a citizen split in two by the lightning?
I am afraid you have never smiled at the hibernation
Of bear cubs except that you saw in it some deep relation

To human suffering and wishes, oh what a bunch of
      crackpots!"
The black-haired man sits down, and the others shoot
      arrows at him.
A blond man stands up and says,
"He is right! Why should we be organized to defend the
      kingdom
Of dullness? There are so many slimy people connected
      with poetry,
Too, and people who know nothing about it!
I am not recommending that poets like each other and
      organize to fight them,
But simply that lightning should strike them."
Then the assembled mediocrities shot arrows at the
      blond-haired man.
The chairman stood up on the platform, oh he was
      physically ugly!
He was small-limbed and -boned and thought he was
      quite seductive,
But he was bald with certain hideous black hairs,
And his voice had the sound of water leaving a vaseline
      bathtub,
And he said, "The subject for this evening's discussion is
      poetry
On the subject of love between swans." And everyone
      threw candy hearts
At the disgusting man, and they stuck to his bib and
      tucker,
And he danced up and down on the platform in terrific
      glee
And recited the poetry of his little friends—but the
      blond man stuck his head

Out of a cloud and recited poems about the east and
    thunder,
And the black-haired man moved through the strato-
    sphere chanting
Poems of the relationships between terrific prehistoric
    charcoal whales,
And the slimy man with candy hearts sticking all over him
Wilted away like a cigarette paper on which the bumble-
    bees have urinated,
And all the professors left the room to go back to their
    duty,
And all that were left in the room were five or six poets
And together they sang the new poem of the twentieth
    century
Which, though influenced by Mallarmé, Shelley, Byron,
    and Whitman,
Plus a million other poets, is still entirely original
And is so exciting that it cannot be here repeated.
You must go to the Poem Society and wait for it to happen.
Once you have heard this poem you will not love any
    other,
Once you have dreamed this dream you will be
    inconsolable,
Once you have loved this dream you will be as one dead,
Once you have visited the passages of this time's great art!

2

"Oh to be seventeen years old
Once again," sang the red-haired man, "and not know
    that poetry
Is ruled with the sceptre of the dumb, the deaf, and the
    creepy!"

And the shouting persons battered his immortal body
    with stones
And threw his primitive comedy into the sea
From which it sang forth poems irrevocably blue.

Who are the great poets of our time, and what are their
    names?
Yeats of the baleful influence, Auden of the baleful
    influence, Eliot of the baleful influence
(Is Eliot a great poet? no one knows), Hardy, Stevens,
    Williams (is Hardy of our time?),
Hopkins (is Hopkins of our time?), Rilke (is Rilke of our
    time?), Lorca (is Lorca of our time?), who is still of
    our time?
Mallarmé, Valéry, Apollinaire, Eluard, Reverdy, French
    poets are still of our time,
Pasternak and Mayakovsky, is Jouve of our time?

Where are young poets in America, they are trembling
    in publishing houses and universities,
Above all they are trembling in universities, they are
    bathing the library steps with their spit,
They are gargling out innocuous (to whom?) poems
    about maple trees and their children,
Sometimes they brave a subject like the Villa d'Este or a
    lighthouse in Rhode Island,
Oh what worms they are! they wish to perfect their form.
Yet could not these young men, put in another profession,
Succeed admirably, say at sailing a ship? I do not doubt
    it, Sir, and I wish we could try them.
(A plane flies over the ship holding a bomb but perhaps
    it will not drop the bomb,

The young poets from the universities are staring anx-
    iously at the skies,
Oh they are remembering their days on the campus
    when they looked up to watch birds excrete,
They are remembering the days they spent making their
    elegant poems.)

Is there no voice to cry out from the wind and say what
    it is like to be the wind,
To be roughed up by the trees and to bring music from
    the scattered houses
And the stones, and to be in such intimate relationship
    with the sea
That you cannot understand it? Is there no one who
    feels like a pair of pants?

3

Summer in the trees! "It is time to strangle several bad
    poets."
The yellow hobbyhorse rocks to and fro, and from the
    chimney
Drops the Strangler! The white and pink roses are
    slightly agitated by the struggle,
But afterwards beside the dead "poet" they cuddle up
    comfortingly against their vase. They are safer now,
    no one will compare them to the sea.

Here on the railroad train, one more time, is the Strangler.
He is going to get that one there, who is on his way to a
    poetry reading.
Agh! Biff! A body falls to the moving floor.

In the football stadium I also see him,
He leaps through the frosty air at the maker of
    comparisons
Between football and life and silently, silently strangles
    him!

Here is the Strangler dressed in a cowboy suit
Leaping from his horse to annihilate the students of myth!
The Strangler's ear is alert for the names of Orpheus,
Cuchulain, Gawain, and Odysseus,
And for poems addressed to Jane Austen, F. Scott
    Fitzgerald,
To Ezra Pound, and to personages no longer living
Even in anyone's thoughts—O Strangler the Strangler!

He lies on his back in the waves of the Pacific Ocean.

4

Supposing that one walks out into the air
On a fresh spring day and has the misfortune
To encounter an article on modern poetry
In *New World Writing*, or has the misfortune
To see some examples of some of the poetry
Written by the men with their eyes on the myth
And the Missus and the midterms, in the *Hudson Review*,
Or, if one is abroad, in *Botteghe Oscure*,
Or indeed in *Encounter*, what is one to do
With the rest of one's day that lies blasted to ruins
All bluely about one, what is one to do?
O surely one cannot complain to the President,
Nor even to the deans of Columbia College,

Nor to T. S. Eliot, nor to Ezra Pound,
And supposing one writes to the Princess Caetani,
"Your poets are awful!" what good would it do?
And supposing one goes to the *Hudson Review*
With a package of matches and sets fire to the building?
One ends up in prison with trial subscriptions
To the *Partisan*, *Sewanee*, and *Kenyon Review*!

5

Sun out! perhaps there is a reason for the lack of poetry
In these ill-contented souls, perhaps they need air!

Blue air, fresh air, come in, I welcome you, you are an
    art student,
Take off your cap and gown and sit down on the chair.

Together we shall paint the poets—but no, air! perhaps
    you should go to them, quickly,
Give them a little inspiration, they need it, perhaps they
    are out of breath,
Give them a little inhuman company before they freeze
    the English language to death!
(And rust their typewriters a little, be sea air! be noxious!
    kill them, if you must, but stop their poetry!
I remember I saw you dancing on the surf on the Côte
    d'Azur,
And I stopped, taking my hat off, but you did not
    remember me,
Then afterwards you came to my room bearing a hand-
    ful of orange flowers
And we were together all through the summer night!)

That we might go away together, it is so beautiful on the
    sea, there are a few white clouds in the sky!

But no, air! you must go . . . Ah, stay!

But she has departed and . . . Ugh! what poisonous
    fumes and clouds! what a suffocating atmosphere!
Cough! whose are these hideous faces I see, what is this
    rigor
Infecting the mind? where are the green Azores,
Fond memories of childhood, and the pleasant orange
    trolleys,
A girl's face, red-white, and her breasts and calves, blue
    eyes, brown eyes, green eyes, Fahrenheit
Temperatures, dandelions, and trains, O blue?!
Wind, wind, what is happening? Wind! I can't see any
    bird but the gull, and I feel it should symbolize . . .
Oh, pardon me, there's a swan, one two three swans, a
    great white swan, hahaha how pretty they are! Smack!
Oh! stop! help! yes, I see—disrespect for my superiors—
    forgive me, dear Zeus, nice Zeus, parabolic bird,
    O feathered excellence! white!
There is Achilles too, and there's Ulysses, I've always
    wanted to see them,
And there is Helen of Troy, I suppose she is Zeus too,
    she's so terribly pretty—hello, Zeus, my you are
    beautiful, Bang!
One more mistake and I get thrown out of the Modern
    Poetry Association, help! Why aren't there any
    adjectives around?

Oh there are, there's practically nothing else—look,
   here's *grey, utter, agonized, total, phenomenal, gracile,
   invidious, sundered,* and *fused,*
Elegant, absolute, pyramidal, and . . . Scream! but what
   can I describe with these words? States!
States symbolized and divided by two, complex states,
   magic states, states of consciousness governed by an
   aroused sincerity, cockadoodle doo!
Another bird! is it morning? Help! where am I? am I in
   the barnyard? oink oink, scratch, moo! Splash!
My first lesson. "Look around you. What do you think
   and feel?" *Uhhh* . . . "Quickly!" *This Connecticut
   landscape would have pleased Vermeer.* Wham! A-Plus.
   "Congratulations!" I am promoted.
OOOhhhhh I wish I were dead, what a headache! My
   second lesson: "Rewrite your first lesson line six
   hundred times. Try to make it into a magnetic
   field." I can do it too. But my poor line! What a
   nightmare! Here comes a tremendous horse,
Trojan, I presume. No, it's my third lesson. "Look, look!
   Watch him, see what he's doing? That's what we
   want you to do. Of course it won't be the same as
   his at first, but . . ." I demur. Is there no other way
   to fertilize minds?
Bang! I give in . . . Already I see my name in two or
   three anthologies, a serving girl comes into the barn
   bringing me the anthologies,
She is very pretty and I smile at her a little sadly, perhaps
   it is my last smile! Perhaps she will hit me! But no,
   she smiles in return, and she takes my hand.

My hand, my hand! what is this strange thing I feel in
my hand, on my arm, on my chest, my face—can it
be . . . ? it is! AIR!

Air, air, you've come back! Did you have any success?
"What do you think?" I don't know, air. You are so
strong, air.

And she breaks my chains of straw, and we walk down
the road, behind us the hideous fumes!

Soon we reach the seaside, she is a young art student
who places her head on my shoulder,

I kiss her warm red lips, and here is the Strangler,
reading the *Kenyon Review*! Good luck to you,
Strangler!

Goodbye, Helen! goodbye, fumes! goodbye, abstracted
dried-up boys! goodbye, dead trees! goodbye,
skunks!

Goodbye, manure! goodbye, critical manicure! goodbye,
you big fat men standing on the east coast as well as
the west giving poems the test! farewell, Valéry's
stern dictum!

Until tomorrow, then, scum floating on the surface of
poetry! goodbye for a moment, refuse that happens
to land in poetry's boundaries! adieu, stale eggs
teaching imbeciles poetry to bolster up your egos!
adios, boring anomalies of these same stale eggs!

Ah, but the scum is deep! Come, let me help you! and
soon we pass into the clear blue water. Oh
GOODBYE, castrati of poetry! farewell, stale pale
skunky pentameters (the only honest English meter,
gloop gloop!) until tomorrow, horrors! oh, farewell!

Hello, sea! good morning, sea! hello, clarity and
    excitement, you great expanse of green—

O green, beneath which all of them shall drown!

The Pleasures of Peace

Another ribald tale of the good times at Madame Lipsky's.
Giorgio Finogle had come in with an imitation of the
    latest Russian poet,
The one who wrote the great "Complaint About the
    Peanut Farm" which I read to you last year at Mrs.
    Riley's,
Do you remember? and then of course Giorgio had
    written this imitation
So he came in with it. . . . Where was I and what was I
    saying?
The big beer parlor was filled with barmaids and men
    named Stuart
Who were all trying to buy a big red pitcher of beer for
    an artiste named Alma Stuart
Whom each claimed as his very own because of the
    similarity in names—
This in essence was Buddy's parody—O Giorgio, you
    idiot, Marian Stuart snapped,
It all has something to do with me! But no, Giorgio
    replied,
Biting in a melancholy way the edge off a cigar-paper-
    patterned envelope

In which he had been keeping the Poem for many days
Waiting to show it to his friends. And actually it's not a
    parody at all,
I just claimed it was, out of embarrassment. It's a poetic
    present for you all,
All of whom I love! Is it capable to love more than one—
    I wonder! Alma cried,
And we went out onto the bicycle-shaped dock where a
    malicious swarm of mosquitoes
Were parlaying after having invaded the old beer parlor.
The men named Stuart were now involved in a fight to
    the death
But the nearer islands lay fair in the white night light.
Shall we embark toward them? I said, placing my hand
    upon one exceedingly gentle
And fine. A picture of hairnets is being projected. Here
Comes someone with Alma Stuart! Is it real, this night?
    Or have we a gentle fantasy?
The Russian poet appears. He seems to consider it real,
    all right. He's
Quite angry. Where's the Capitalist fairy that put me
    down? he squirts
At our nomadic simplicity. "Complaint About the
    Peanut Farm" is a terrific poem. Yes,
In a way, yes. The Hairdresser of Night engulfs them all
    in foam.

"I love your work, *The Pleasures of Peace*," the Professor
    said to me next day;
"I think it adequately encompasses the hysteria of our era
And puts certain people in their rightful place. Chapeau!
    Bravo!"

"You don't get it," I said. "I like all this. I called this
    poem
Pleasures of Peace because I'm not sure they will be lasting!
I wanted people to be able to see what these pleasures
    are
That they may come back to them." "But they are all so
    hysterical, so—so transitory,"
The critic replied. "I mean, how can you—what kind of
    pleasures are these?
They seem more like pains to me—if I may say what I
    mean."
"Well, I don't know, Professor," I said; "permanent joys
Have so far been denied this hysterical person. Though
    I confess
Far other joys I've had and will describe in time.
And then too there's the pleasure of *writing* these—
    perhaps to experience is not the same."
The Professor paused, lightly, upon the temple stair.
"I will mention you among the immortals, Ken," he said,
"Because you have the courage of what you believe.
But there I will never mention those sniveling rats
Who only claim to like these things because they're
    fashionable."
"Professor!" I cried, "My darling! my dream!" And she
    stripped, and I saw there
Creamy female marble, the waist and thighs of which I
    had always dreamed.
"Professor! Loved one! why the disguise?" "It was a test,"
    she said,
"Of which you have now only passed the first portion.
You must write More, and More—"

26

"And be equally persuasive?" I questioned, but She
Had vanished through the Promontory door.

So now I must devote my days to The Pleasures of
        Peace—
To my contemporaries I'll leave the Horrors of War,
They can do them better than I—each poet shares only
        a portion
Of the vast Territory of Rhyme. Here in Peace shall I
        stake out
My temporal and permanent claim. But such silver as I
        find
I will give to the Universe—the gold I'll put in other
        poems.
Thus in time there'll be a mountain range of gold
Of considerable interest. Oh may you come back in time
And in my lifetime to see it, most perfect and most
        delectable reader!
We poets in our youth begin with fantasies,
But then at least we think they may be realities—
The poems we create in our age
Require your hand upon our shoulder, your eye on our
        page.

Here are listed all the Pleasures of Peace that there
        could possibly be.
Among them are the pleasures of Memory (which
        Delmore Schwartz celebrated), the pleasures of
        autonomy,
The pleasures of agoraphobia and the sudden release
Of the agoraphobic person from the identified market-
        place, the pleasures of roving over you

And rolling over the beach, of being in a complicated
    car, of sleeping,
Of drawing ropes with you, of planning a deranged
    comic strip, of shifting knees
At the accelerator pump, of blasphemy, of cobra settle-
    ment in a dilapidated skin country
Without clops, and therefore every pleasure is also
    included; which, after these—

Oh Norman Robinson, the airplane, the village, the
    batteries,
All this I remember, the Cheese-o-Drome, the phallic
    whips, the cucumbers,
The ginger from Australia, the tiny whorehouses no
    bigger than a phallus's door,
The evenings without any cucumbers, the phallus's
    people,
The old men trailing blue lassos from door to door,
Who are they all, anyway? I was supposed to be on my
    way to Boston
To go to college or get elected to the Legislature
And now I'm here with a lot of cowboys who talk
    spiritual Dutch! Let
Me out of here! The lumberyard smelled of the sweet
    calla lilies
The courtyard was fragrant with thyme. I released your
    hand
And walked into the Mexicana Valley, where my father
    was first a cowboy.
I take a genuine interest in the people of this country

Yes sir I think you might even call me Coleman the
      Dutch but now the night sky fills with fairies
It is all that modern stuff beginning to happen again,
      well, let it—

We robots tell the truth about old Gabby
But when the shirtfront scuffs we yell for Labby
It is a scientific stunt
Which Moonlight has brought you from Australia
Sit it down on this chair shaped like a pirate
When you have come three times I will give you a silver-
      ware hazelnut
With which you can escape from time
For this I'm calling in all the poets who take dope
To help me out, here they come
Oh is there room in the universe for such as we?
They say, but though we cannot make our Time
Stand still, yet we'll him silver like a Dime.
Inversions yet! and not even sexual ones!
O Labrador, you are the sexual Pennsylvania of our
      times!

Chapter Thirty Seven.
On the Planisphere everyone was having a nut
When suddenly my Lulu appeared.
She was a big broad about six feet seven
And she had a red stone in her ear
Which was stringent in its beauty.
I demanded at once the removal of people from the
      lobby
So we could begin to down ABC tablets and start to feel
      funny

But Mordecai La Schlomp our Leader replied that we
    did not need any
That a person could feel good without any artificial
    means.
Oh the Pleasures of Peace are infinite and they cannot
    be counted—
One single piece of pink mint chewing gum contains
    more pleasures
Than the whole rude gallery of war! And the moon
    passes by
In an otherwise undistinguished lesson on the geography
    of this age
Which has had fifty-seven good lovers and ninety-six
    wars. By Giorgio Finogle.

It turns out that we're competing for the Peace Award,
Giorgio Finogle and I. We go into the hair parlor, the
    barber—
We get to talking about war and about peace.
The barber feels that we are really good people at heart
Even though his own views turn out to be conservative.
"I've read Finogle's piece, the part of it that was in
    Smut," he
Says, "and I liked it. Yours, Koch, I haven't yet seen,
But Alyne and Francie told me that you were the better
    poet."
"I don't know," I said. "Giorgio is pretty good." And
    Giorgio comes back from the bathroom
Now, with a grin on his face. "I've got an idea for my
Pleasures of Peace," he says, "I'm going to make it include
Each person in the universe discussing their own bag—

Translation, their main interest, and what they want to
    be—"
"You'll never finish it, Giorgio," I said. "At least I'll
Get started," he replied, and he ran out of the barbershop.

In the quiet night we take turns riding horseback and
    falling asleep.
Your breasts are more beautiful than a gold mine.
I think I'll become a professional man.
The reason we are up-to-date is we're some kind of
    freaks.
I don't know what to tell the old man
But he is concerned with two kinds of phenomena and I
    am interested in neither. What *are* you interested in?
Being some kind of freaks, I think. Let's go to
    Transylvania.
I don't understand your buddy all the time. Who?
The one with HANDLEBAR written across his head.
He's a good guy, he just doesn't see the difference be-
    tween a man and a bike. If I love you
It's because you belong to and have a sublime tolerance
For such people. Yes, but in later life, I mean—
It is Present Life we've got to keep up on the screen,
Isn't it. Well yes, she said, but—
I am very happy that you are interested in it. The
    French poodle stopped being Irish entirely
And we are all out of the other breeds.
The society woman paused, daintily, upon the hotel stair.
No, I must have a poodle, said she; not an Irish setter
Would satisfy me in my mad passion for the poodle
    breeds!

As usual, returning to the bed
I find that you are inside it and sound asleep. I smile
happily and look at your head.
It is regular-size and has beautiful blonde hair all
around it.
Some is lying across the pillow. I touch it with my feet
Then leap out the window into the public square,
And I tune my guitar.
"O Mistress Mine, where are you roving?" That's my
tune! roars Finogle, and he
Comes raging out of the *Beefsteak*—I was going to put
that in MY Pleasures of Peace.
Oh normal comportment! even you too I shall include in
the Pleasures of Peace,
And you, relative humidity five hundred and sixty-two
degrees!
But what of you, poor sad glorious aqueduct
Of boorish ashes made by cigarettes smoked at the
Cupcake
Award—And Sue Ellen Musgrove steps on one of my
feet. "Hello!"
She says. "You're that famous COKE, aren't you,
That no one can drink? When are you going to give us
your famous Iliad
That everyone's been talking of, I mean your Pleasures
of Peace!"

Life changes as the universe changes, but the universe
changes
More slowly, as bedevilments increase.
Sunlight comes through a clot for example

Which Zoo Man has thrown on the floor. It is the Night
    of the Painted Pajamas
And the Liberals are weeping for peace. The
    Conservatives are raging for it.
The Independents are staging a parade. And we are
    completely naked
Walking through the bedroom for peace. I have this
    friend who had myopia
So he always had to get very close to people
And girls thought he was trying to make out—
Why didn't he get glasses?—He was a Pacifist! The
    Moon shall overcome!

Outside in the bar yard the Grecians are screaming for
    peace
And the Alsatians, the Albanians, the Alesians, the
    Rubans, the Aleutians,
And the Iranians, all, all are screaming for peace.
They shall win it, their peace, because I am going to
    help them!
And he leaped out the window for peace!
Headline: GIORGIO FINOGLE,
NOTED POET, LAST NIGHT LEAPED OUT THE
    WINDOW FOR PEACE.
ASIDE FROM HEAD INJURIES HIS CONDITION
    IS REPORTED NORMAL.
But Giorgio never was normal! Oh the horrors of peace,
I mean of peace-fighting! But Giorgio is all right,
He is still completely himself. "I am going to throw this
    hospital
Bed out the window for peace," when we see him, he says.

And, "Well, I guess your poem will be getting way ahead
    of mine now," he says
Sadly, ripping up an envelope for peace and weakly
    holding out his hand
For my girl, Ellen, to stroke it; "I will no longer be the
    most famous poet
For peace. You will, and you know it." "But you jumped
    out the
Window, Finogle," I said, "and your deed shall live longer
In men's imaginations than any verse." But he looked at
    the sky
Through the window's beautiful eye and he said,
    "Kenneth, I have not written one word
Of my Poem for Peace for three weeks. I've struck a snarl
And that's why (I believe) I jumped out the
Window—pure poetic frustration. Now tell them all
    that, how
They'll despise me, oh sob sob—" "Giorgio," I said,
    trying to calm him down but laughing
So hard I could barely digest the dinner of imagination
In which your breasts were featured as on a Popeye card
When winter has lighted the lanterns and the falls are
    asleep
Waiting for next day's shards, "Giorgio," I said, "the
    pleasures—"
But hysteria transported us all.

When I awoke you were in a star-shaped muffin, I was in
    a loaf of bread
Shaped like a camera, and Giorgio was still in his
    hospital bed

But a huge baker loomed over us. One false moof and I
     die you! he said
In a murderous throaty voice and I believe in the yellow
     leaves, the
Orange, the red leaves of autumn, the tan leaves, and the
     promoted ones
Of green, of green and blue. Sometimes walking
     through an ordinary garden
You will see a bird, and the overcoat will fall from your
Shoulders, slightly, exposing one beautiful curve
On which sunbeams alighting forget to speak a single
     word
To their parent sun and are thus cut off
Without a heating unit, but need none being on your
     breast
Which I have re-christened "Loaves" for the beginning
     of this year
In which I hope the guns won't fire any more, the baker
     sang
To his baker lady, and then he had totally disappeared.
It looks as though everyone were going to be on our
     side!

And the flowers came out, and they were on our side,
Even the yellow little ones that grow beside your door
And the huge orange ones were bending to one side
As we walked past them, I looked into your blue eyes
And I said, "If we come out of this door
Any more, let it be to enter only this nervous paradise
Of peaceful living conditions, and if Giorgio is roped
     down

Let them untie him, so he can throw his hospital bed out
the door
For all we need besides peace, which is considerable, but
first we need that—"

Daredevil, Julian and Maddalo, and John L. Lewis
Are running down the stairways for peace, they are
gathering the ice
And throwing it in buckets, they are raising purple
parasols for peace
And on top of these old sunlight sings her song, "New
lights, old lights again, blue lights for peace,
Red lights for the low, insulted parasol, and a few
crutches thrown around for peace"—
Oh contentment is the key
To continuing exploration of the nations and their feet;
Therefore, andiamo—the footfall is waiting in the car
And peaceful are the markets and the sneaks;
Peaceful are the Garfinkle ping-pong balls
And peaceful are the blooms beneath the sea
Peaceful are the unreserved airplane loops and the popu-
larly guided blips
Also the Robert Herrick stone sings a peaceful song
And the banana factory is getting hip, and the pigs'
Easter party too is beginning to join in a general
celebration
And the women and men of old Peru and young Haifa
and ancient Japan and beautiful young rippling
Lake Tahoe
And hairy old Boston and young Freeport and young
Santo Domingo and old father Candelabra the
Chieftain of Hoboes

Are rolling around the parapets for peace, and now the
    matadors are throwing in
Huge blops of canvas and the postgraduates are filling in
As grocery dates at peanut dances and the sunlight is
    filling in
Every human world canvas with huge and luminous
    pleasure gobs of peace—
And the Tintorettos are looking very purple for peace
And the oyster campus is beginning its peaceful song—

Oh let it be concluded, including the medals!
Peace will come thrusting out of the sky
Tomorrow morning, to bomb us into quietude.
For a while we can bid goodbye
To the frenesies of this poem, The Pleasures of Peace.
When there is peace we will not need anything but bread
Stars and plaster with which to begin.
Roaming from one beard to another we shall take the tin
From the mines and give it to roaring Fidel Castro.
Where Mao Tse Tung lies buried in ocean fields of
    sleeping cars
Our Lorcaesque decisions will clonk him out
And resurrect him to the rosebuddy sky
Of early evening. And the whip-shaped generals of Hanoi
Shall be taken in overcoats to visit the sky
And the earth will be gasping for joy!
"A wonder!" "A rout!" "No need now for any further
    poems!" "A Banzai for peace!" "He can speak to us
    all!"
And "Great, man!" "Impressive!" "Something new for
    you, Ken!" "Astounding!" "A real

Epic!" "The worst poem I have ever read!" "Abominably
　　tasteless!" "Too funny!" "Dead, man!
A cop out! a real white man's poem! a folderol of honky
　　blank spitzenburger smugglerout Caucasian gyp
Of phony bourgeois peace poetry, a total shrig!"
　　"Terrific!" "I will expect you at six!"
"A lovely starry catalogue for peace!" "Is it Shakespeare
　　or Byron who breathes
In the lines of his poem?" "You have given us the
　　Pleasures of Peace,
Now where is the real thing?" "Koch has studied his
　　history!" "Bold!" "Stunning!" "It touches us like
　　leaves
Sparkling in April—but is that all there is
To his peace plea?" Well, you be the one
To conclude it, if you think it needs more—I want to
　　end it,
I want to see real Peace again! Oh peace bams!
I need your assistance—and peace drams, distilling
　　through the world! peace lamps, be shining! and
　　peace lambs, rumble up the shore!
O Goddess, sweet Muse, I'm stopping—now show us
　　where you are!

And the big boats come sailing into the harbor for peace
And the little apes are running around the jungle for
　　peace
And the day (that is, the star of day, the sun) is shining
　　for peace
Somewhere a moustachioed student is puzzling over the
　　works of Raymond Roussel for peace
And the Mediterranean peach tees are fast asleep for
　　peace

With their pink arms akimbo and the blue plums of
     Switzerland for peace
And the monkeys are climbing for coconuts and peace
The Hawaiian palm
And serpents are writhing for peace—those are snakes—
And the Alps, Mount Vesuvius, all the really big
     important mountains
Are rising for peace, and they're filled with rocks—
     surely it won't be long;
And Leonardo da Vinci's *Last Supper* is moving across
     the monastery wall
A few micrometers for peace, and Paolo Uccello's red
     horses
Are turning a little redder for peace, and the Anglo-
     Saxon dining hall
Begins glowing like crazy, and Beowulf, Robert E. Lee,
     Sir Barbarossa, and Baron Jeep
Are sleeping on the railways for peace and darting
     around the harbor
And leaping into the sailboats and the sailboats will go on
And underneath the sailboats the sea will go on and we
     will go on
And the birds will go on and the snappy words will go on
And the tea sky and the sloped marine sky
And the hustle of beans will go on and the unserious
     canoe
It will all be going on in connection with you, peace, and
     my poem, like a Cadillac of wampum
Unredeemed and flying madly, will go exploding through
New cities sweet inflated, planispheres, ingenious hair, a
     camera smashing

Badinage, cerebral stands of atmospheres, unequaled,
    dreamed of
Empeacements, candled piers, fumisteries, emphatic
    moods, terrestialism's
Crackle, love's flat, sun's sweets, oh Peace, to you.

The Circus

I remember when I wrote The Circus
I was living in Paris, or rather we were living in Paris
Janice, Frank was alive, the Whitney Museum
Was still on 8th Street, or was it still something else?
Fernand Léger lived in our building
Well it wasn't really our building it was the building we
    lived in
Next to a Grand Guignol troupe who made a lot of noise
So that one day I yelled through a hole in the wall
Of our apartment I don't know why there was a hole there
Shut up! And the voice came back to me saying something
I don't know what. Once I saw Léger walk out of the
    building
I think. Stanley Kunitz came to dinner. I wrote The Circus
In two tries, the first getting most of the first stanza;
That fall I also wrote an opera libretto called Louisa or
    Matilda.
Jean-Claude came to dinner. He said (about "cocktail
    sauce")
It should be good on something but not on these
    (oysters).
By that time I think I had already written The Circus.

Part of the inspiration came while walking to the post
        office one night
And I wrote a big segment of The Circus
When I came back, having been annoyed to have to go
I forget what I went there about
You were back in the apartment what a dump actually we
        liked it
I think with your hair and your writing and the pans
Moving strummingly about the kitchen and I wrote The
        Circus
It was a summer night no it was an autumn one summer
        when
I remember it but actually no autumn that black dusk
        toward the post office
And I wrote many other poems then but The Circus was
        the best
Maybe not by far the best Geography was also wonderful
And the Airplane Betty poems (inspired by you) but The
        Circus was the best.

Sometimes I feel I actually am the person
Who did this, who wrote that, including that poem The
        Circus
But sometimes on the other hand I don't.
There are so many factors engaging our attention!
At every moment the happiness of others, the health of
        those we know and our own!
And the millions upon millions of people we don't know
        and their well-being to think about
So it seems strange I found time to write The Circus
And even spent two evenings on it, and that I have also
        the time

To remember that I did it, and remember you and me
　　then, and write this poem about it
At the beginning of The Circus
The Circus girls are rushing through the night
In the circus wagons and tulips and other flowers will be
　　picked
A long time from now this poem wants to get off on its
　　own
Someplace like a painting not held to a depiction of
　　composing The Circus.

Noel Lee was in Paris then but usually out of it
In Germany or Denmark giving a concert
As part of an endless activity
Which was either his career or his happiness or a combi-
　　nation of both
Or neither I remember his dark eyes looking he was
　　nervous
With me perhaps because of our days at Harvard.

It is understandable enough to be nervous with anybody!

How softly and easily one feels when alone
Love of one's friends when one is commanding the time
　　and space syndrome
If that's the right word which I doubt but together how
　　come one is so nervous?
One is not always but what was I then and what am I
　　now attempting to create
If create is the right word
Out of this combination of experience and aloneness

And who are you telling me it is or is not a poem (not
      you)? Go back with me though
To those nights I was writing The Circus.
Do you like that poem? have you read it? It is in my
      book Thank You
Which Grove just reprinted. I wonder how long I am
      going to live
And what the rest will be like I mean the rest of my life.

John Cage said to me the other night How old are you?
      and I told him forty-six
(Since then I've become forty-seven) he said
Oh that's a great age I remember.
John Cage once told me he didn't charge much for his
      mushroom identification course (at the New School)
Because he didn't want to make a profit from nature

He was ahead of his time I was behind my time we were
      both in time
Brilliant go to the head of the class and "time is a river"
It doesn't seem like a river to me it seems like an
      unformed plan
Days go by and still nothing is decided about
What to do until you know it never will be and then you
      say "time"
But you really don't care much about it any more
Time means something when you have the major part of
      yours ahead of you
As I did in Aix-en-Provence that was three years before I
      wrote The Circus
That year I wrote Bricks and The Great Atlantic Rainway

I felt time surround me like a blanket endless and soft
I could go to sleep endlessly and wake up and still be in it
But I treasured secretly the part of me that was individu-
ally changing
Like Noel Lee I was interested in my career
And still am but now it is like a town I don't want to
leave
Not a tower I am climbing opposed by ferocious enemies

I never mentioned my friends in my poems at the time I
wrote The Circus
Although they meant almost more than anything to me
Of this now for some time I've felt an attenuation
So I'm mentioning them maybe this will bring them
back to me
Not them perhaps but what I felt about them
John Ashbery Jane Freilicher Larry Rivers Frank O'Hara
Their names alone bring tears to my eyes
As seeing Polly did last night
It is beautiful at any time but the paradox is leaving it
In order to feel it when you've come back the sun has
declined
And the people are merrier or else they've gone home
altogether
And you are left alone well you put up with that your
sureness is like the sun
While you have it but when you don't its lack's a black
and icy night. I came home
And wrote The Circus that night, Janice. I didn't come
and speak to you
And put my arm around you and ask you if you'd like to
take a walk

Or go to the Cirque Medrano though that's what I wrote
    poems about
And am writing about that now, and now I'm alone

And this is not as good a poem as The Circus
And I wonder if any good will come of either of them all
    the same.

Alive for an Instant

I have a bird in my head and a pig in my stomach
And a flower in my genitals and a tiger in my genitals
And a lion in my genitals and I am after you but I have a
    song in my heart
And my song is a dove
I have a man in my hands I have a woman in my shoes
I have a landmark decision in my reason
I have a death rattle in my nose I have summer in my
    brain water
This is the matter with me and the hammer of my
    mother and father
Who created me with everything
But I lack calm I lack rose
Though I do not lack extreme delicacy of rose petal
Who is it that I wish to astonish?
In the birdcall I found a reminder of you
But it was thin and brittle and gone in an instant
Has nature set out to be a great entertainer?
Obviously not A great reproducer? A great Nothing?
Well I will leave that up to you

I have a knocking woodpecker in my heart and I think I
    have three souls
One for love one for poetry and one for acting out my
    insane self
Not insane but boring but perpendicular but untrue but
    true
The three rarely sing together take my hand it's active
The active ingredient in it is a touch
I am Lord Byron I am Percy Shelley I am Ariosto
I eat the bacon I went down the slide I have a thunder-
    storm in my inside I will never hate you
But how can this maelstrom be appealing? do you like
    menageries? my god
Most people want a man! So here I am
I have a pheasant in my reminders I have a goshawk in
    my clouds
Whatever is it which has led all these animals to you?
A resurrection? or maybe an insurrection? an
    inspiration?
I have a baby in my landscape and I have a wild rat in my
    secrets from you.

Some General Instructions

Do not bake bread in an oven that is not made of stone
Or you risk having imperfect bread. Byron wrote,
"The greatest pleasure in life is drinking hock
And soda water the morning after, when one has
A hangover," or words to that effect. It is a
Pleasure, for me, of the past. I do not drink so much

Any more. And when I do, I am not in sufficiently good
Shape to enjoy the hock and seltzer in the morning.
I am envious of this pleasure as I think of it. Do not
You be envious. In fact I cannot tell envy
From wish and desire and sharing imperfectly
What others have got and not got. But *envy* is a good
    word
To use, as *hate* is, and *lust*, because they make their point
In the worst and most direct way, so that as a
Result one is able to deal with them and go on one's way.
I read *Don Juan* twenty years ago, and six years later
I wrote a poem in emulation of it. I began
Searching for another stanza but gave in
To the ottava rima after a while, after I'd tried
Some practice stanzas in it; it worked so well
It was too late to stop, it seemed to me. Do not
Be in too much of a hurry to emulate what
You admire. Sometimes it may take a number of years
Before you are ready, but there it is, building
Inside you, a constructing egg. Low-slung
Buildings are sometimes dangerous to walk in and
Out of. A building should be at least one foot and a half
Above one's height, so that if one leaps
In surprise or joy or fear, one's head will not be injured.
Very high ceilings such as those in Gothic
Churches are excellent for giving a spiritual feeling.
Low roofs make one feel like a mole in general. But
Smallish rooms can be cozy. Many tiny people
In a little room make an amusing sight. Large
Persons, both male and female, are best seen out of doors.
Ships sided against a canal's side may be touched and
Patted, but sleeping animals should not be, for

They may bite, in anger and surprise. Of all animals
The duck is seventeenth lowliest, the eagle not as high
On the list as one would imagine, rating
Only ninety-fifth. The elephant is either two or four
Depending on the author of the list, and the tiger
Is seven. The lion is three or six. Blue is the
Favorite color of many people because the sky
Is blue and the sea is blue and many people's eyes
Are blue, but blue is not popular in those countries
Where it is the color of mold. In Spain blue
Symbolizes cowardice. In America it symbolizes
    "Americanness."
The racial mixture in North America should
Not be misunderstood. The English came here first,
And the Irish and the Germans and the Dutch. There
    were
Some French here also. The Russians, the Jews, and
The Blacks came afterwards. The women are only
    coming now
To a new kind of prominence in America, where
    Liberation
Is their byword. Giraffes, which people ordinarily
Associate with Africa, can be seen in many urban zoos
All over the world. They are an adaptable animal,
As Greek culture was an adaptable culture. Rome
Spread it all over the world. You should know,
Before it did, Alexander spread it as well. Read
As many books as you can without reading interfering
With your time for living. Boxing was formerly illegal
In England, and also, I believe, in America. If
You feel a law is unjust, you may work to change it.
It is not true, as many people say, that

That is just the way things are. Or, Those are the rules,
Immutably. The rules can be changed, although
It may be a slow process. When decorating a window, you
Should try to catch the eye of the passer-by, then
Hold it; he or she should become constantly more
Absorbed in what is being seen. Stuffed animal toys
     should be
Fluffy and a pleasure to hold in the hands. They
Should not be too resistant, nor should they be made
With any poisonous materials. Be careful not to set fire
To a friend's house. When covering over
A gas stove with paper or inflammable plastic
So you can paint the kitchen without injuring the stove,
Be sure there is no pilot light, or that it is out.
Do not take pills too quickly when you think you have a
     cold
Or other minor ailment, but wait and see if it
Goes away by itself, as many processes do
Which are really part of something else, not
What we suspected. Raphael's art is no longer as popular
As it was fifty years ago, but an aura
Still hangs about it, partly from its former renown.
The numbers seven and eleven are important to remem-
     ber in dice
As are the expressions "hard eight," "Little Joe," and
     "fever,"
Which means *five*. Girls in short skirts when they
Kneel to play dice are beautiful, and even if they
Are not very rich or good rollers, may be
Pleasant as a part of the game. Saint Ursula
And her eleven thousand virgins has
Recently been discovered to be a printer's mistake;

There were only eleven virgins, not eleven thousand.
This makes it necessary to append a brief explanation
When speaking of Apollinaire's parody *Les*
Onze Mille Verges, which means eleven thousand
Male sexual organs—or sticks, for beating. It is a porno-
       graphic book.
Sexual information should be obtained while one is
       young
Enough to enjoy it. To learn of cunnilingus at fifty
Argues a wasted life. One may be tempted to
Rush out into the streets of Hong Kong or
Wherever one is and try to do too much all in one day.
Birds should never be chased out of a nature sanctuary
And shot. Do not believe the beauty of people's faces
Is a sure indication of virtue. The days of
Allegory are over. The Days of Irony are here.
Irony and Deception. But do not harden your heart.
       Remain
Kind and flexible. Travel a lot. By all means
Go to Greece. Meet persons of various social
Orders. Morocco should be visited by foot,
Siberia by plane. Do not be put off by
Thinking of mortality. You live long enough. There
Would, if you lived longer, never be any new
People. Enjoy the new people you see. Put your hand out
And touch that girl's arm. If you are
Able to, have children. When taking pills, be sure
You know what they are. Avoid cholesterol. In
       conversation
Be understanding and witty, in order that you may give
Comfort and excitement at the same time. This is the
       high road to popularity

And social success, but it is also good
For your soul and for your sense of yourself. Be sup-
    portive of others
At the expense of your wit, not otherwise. No
Joke is worth hurting someone deeply. Avoid contagious
    diseases.
If you do not have money, you must probably earn some
But do it in a way that is pleasant and does
Not take too much time. Painting ridiculous pictures
Is one good way, and giving lectures about yourself is
    another.
I once had the idea of importing tropical birds
From Africa to America, but the test cage of birds
All died on the ship, so I was unable to become
Rich that way. Another scheme I had was
To translate some songs from French into English, but
No one wanted to sing them. Living outside Florence
In February, March, and April was an excellent idea
For me, and may be for you, although I recently revisited
The place where I lived, and it is now more "built up";
Still, a little bit further out, it is not, and the fruit trees
There seem the most beautiful in the world. Every day
A new flower would appear in the garden, or every other
    day,
And I was able to put all this in what I wrote. I let
The weather and the landscape be narrative in me. To
    make money
By writing, though, was difficult. So I taught
English in a university in spite of my fear that
I knew nothing. Do not let your fear of ignorance keep
    you
From teaching, if that would be good for you, nor

Should you let your need for success interfere with what
        you love,
In fact, to do. Things have a way of working out
Which is nonsensical, and one should try to see
How that process works. If you can understand chance,
You will be lucky, for luck is what chance is about
To become, in a human context, either
Good luck or bad. You should visit places that
Have a lot of savor for you. You should be glad
To be alive. You must try to be as good as you can.
I do not know what virtue is in an absolute way,
But in the particular it is excellence which does not harm
The material but ennobles and refines it. So, honesty
Ennobles the heart and harms not the person or the coins
He remembers to give back. So, courage ennobles the
        heart
And the bearer's body; and tenderness refines the touch.
The problem of being good and also doing what one
        wishes
Is not as difficult as it seems. It is, however,
Best to get embarked early on one's dearest desires.
Be attentive to your dreams. They are usually about sex,
But they deal with other things as well in an indirect
        fashion
And contain information that you should have.
You should also read poetry. Do not eat too many
        bananas.
In the springtime, plant. In the autumn, harvest.
In the summer and winter, exercise. Do not put
Your finger inside a clam shell or
It may be snapped off by the living clam. Do not wear a
        shirt

More than two times without sending it to the laundry.
Be a bee fancier only if you have a face net. Avoid flies,
Hornets, and wasps. Clasp other people's hands firmly
When you are introduced to them. Say "I am glad to
    meet you!"
Be able to make a mouth and cheeks like a fish. It
Is entertaining. Speaking in accents
Can also entertain people. But do not think
Mainly of being entertaining. Think of your death.
Think of the death of the fish you just imitated. Be
    artistic, and be unfamiliar.
Think of the blue sky, how artists have
Imitated it. Think of your secretest thoughts,
How poets have imitated them. Think of what you feel
Secretly, and how music has imitated that. Make a moue.
Get faucets for every water outlet in your
House. You may like to spend some summers on
An island. Buy woolen material in Scotland and have
The cloth cut in London, lapels made in France.
Become religious when you are tired of everything
Else. As a little old man or woman, die
In a fine and original spirit that is yours alone.
When you are dead, waste, and make room for the future.
Do not make tea from water which is already boiling.
Use the water just as it starts to boil. Otherwise
It will not successfully "draw" the tea, or
The tea will not successfully "draw" it. Byron
Wrote that no man under thirty should ever see
An ugly woman, suggesting desire should be so strong
It affected the princeliest of senses; and Schopenhauer
Suggested the elimination of the human species

As the way to escape from the Will, which he saw as a
    monstrous
Demon-like force which destroys us. When
Pleasure is mild, you should enjoy it, and
When it is violent, permit it, as far as
You can, to enjoy you. Pain should be
Dealt with as efficiently as possible. To "cure" a dead
    octopus
You hold it by one leg and bang it against a rock.
This makes a noise heard all around the harbor,
But it is necessary, for otherwise the meat would be too
    tough.
Fowl are best plucked by humans, but machines
Are more humanitarian, since extended chicken
Plucking is an unpleasant job. Do not eat unwashed beets
Or rare pork, nor should you gobble uncooked dough.
Fruits, vegetables, and cheese make an excellent diet.
You should understand some science. Electricity
Is fascinating. Do not be defeated by the
Feeling that there is too much for you to know. That
Is a myth of the oppressor. You are
Capable of understanding life. And it is yours alone
And only this time. Someone who excites you
Should be told so, and loved, if you can, but no one
Should be able to shake you so much that you wish to
Give up. The sensations you feel are caused by outside
Phenomena and inside impulses. Whatever you
Experience is both "a person out there" and a dream
As well as unwashed electrons. It is your task to see this
    through
To a conclusion that makes sense to all concerned

And that reflects credit on this poem, your species, and
    yourself.
Now go. You cannot come back until these lessons are
    learned
And you can show that you have learned them for
    yourself.

The Art ot Poetry

To write a poem, perfect physical condition
Is desirable but not necessary. Keats wrote
In poor health, as did D. H. Lawrence. A combination
Of disease and old age is an impediment to writing, but
Neither is, alone, unless there is arteriosclerosis—that is,
Hardening of the arteries—but that we shall count as a
    disease
Accompanying old age and therefore a negative
    condition.
Mental health is certainly not a necessity for the
Creation of poetic beauty, but a degree of it
Would seem to be, except in rare cases. Schizophrenic
    poetry
Tends to be loose, disjointed, uncritical of itself, in some
    ways
Like what is best in our modern practice of the poetic art
But unlike it in others, in its lack of concern
For intensity and nuance. A few great poems
By poets supposed to be "mad" are of course known to
    us all,

Such as those of Christopher Smart, but I wonder how
    crazy they were,
These poets who wrote such contraptions of exigent art?
As for Blake's being "crazy," that seems to me very
    unlikely.

But what about Wordsworth? Not crazy, I mean, but
    what about his later work, boring
To the point of inanity, almost, and the destructive
    "corrections" he made
To his *Prelude*, as it nosed along, through the shallows
    of art?
He was really terrible after he wrote the "Ode:
Intimations of Immortality from Recollections of Early
    Childhood," for the most part,
Or so it seems to me. Walt Whitman's "corrections,"
    too, of the *Leaves of Grass*,
And especially "Song of Myself," are almost always
    terrible.

Is there some way to ride to old age and to fame and
    acceptance
And pride in oneself and the knowledge society approves
    one
Without getting lousier and lousier and depleted of
    talent? Yes,
Yeats shows it could be. And Sophocles wrote poetry
    until he was a hundred and one,
Or a hundred, anyway, and drank wine and danced all
    night,
But he was an Ancient Greek and so may not help us
    here. On

The other hand, he may. There is, it would seem, a sense
In which one must grow and develop, and yet stay
          young—
Not peroxide, not stupid, not transplanting hair to look
          peppy,
But young in one's heart. And for this it is a good idea to
          have some
Friends who write as well as you do, who know what you
          are doing,
And know when you are doing something wrong.
They should have qualities that you can never have,
To keep you continually striving up an impossible hill.
These friends should supply such competition as will
          make you, at times, very uncomfortable.
And you should take care of your physical body as well
As of your poetic heart, since consecutive hours of
          advanced concentration
Will be precious to your writing and may not be possible
If you are exhausted and ill. Sometimes an abnormal or
          sick state
Will be inspiring, and one can allow oneself a certain
          number,
But they should not be the rule. Drinking alcohol is all
          right
If not in excess, and I would doubt that it would be
          beneficial
During composition itself. As for marijuana, there are
          those who
Claim to be able to write well under its influence
But I have yet to see the first evidence for such claims.
Stronger drugs are ludicrously inappropriate, since they
          destroy judgment

And taste, and make one either like or dislike everything
    one does,
Or else turn life into a dream. One does not write well
    in one's sleep.

As for following fashionable literary movements,
It is almost irresistible, and for a while I can see no harm
    in it,
But the sooner you find your own style the better off
    you will be.
Then all "movements" fit into it. You have an
    "exercycle" of your own.
Trying out all kinds of styles and imitating poets you like
And incorporating anything valuable you may find there,
These are sound procedures, and in fact I think even
    essential
To the perfection of an original style which is yours alone.
An original style may not last more than four years,
Or even three or even two, sometimes on rare occasions
    one,
And then you must find another. It is conceivable even
    that a style
For a very exigent poet would be for one work only,
After which it would be exhausted, limping, unable to
    sustain any wrong or right.
By "exigent" I mean extremely careful, wanting each
    poem to be a conclusion
Of everything he senses, feels, and knows.
The exigent poet has his satisfactions, which are rela-
    tively special,
But that is not the only kind of poet you can be. There is
    a pleasure in being Venus,

In sending love to everyone, in being Zeus,
In sending thunder to everyone, in being Apollo
And every day sending out light. It is a pleasure to write
    continually
And well, and that is a special poetic dream
Which you may have or you may not. Not all writers
    have it.
Browning once wrote a poem every day of one year
And found it "didn't work out well." But who knows?
He went on for a year—something must have been
    working out.
And why only one poem a day? Why not several? Why
    not one every hour for eight to ten hours a day?
There seems no reason not to try it if you have the
    inclination.

Some poets like "saving up" for poems, others like to
    spend incessantly what they have.
In spending, of course, you get more, there is a "bottom-
    less pocket"
Principle involved, since your feelings are changing
    every instant
And the language has millions of words, and the number
    of combinations is infinite.
True, one may feel, perhaps Puritanically, that
One person can only have so much to say, and, besides,
    ten thousand poems per annum
Per person would flood the earth and perhaps eventually
    the universe,
And one would not want so many poems—so there is a
    "quota system"

Secretly, or not so secretly, at work. "If I can write one
    good poem a year,
I am grateful," the noted Poet says, or "six" or "three."
    Well, maybe for that Poet,
But for you, fellow paddler, and for me, perhaps not.
    Besides, I think poems
Are esthetecologically harmless and psychodegradable
And never would they choke the spirits of the world. For
    a poem only affects us
And "exists," really, if it is worth it, and there can't be
    too many of those.
Writing constantly, in any case, is the poetic dream
Diametrically opposed to the "ultimate distillation"
Dream, which is that of the exigent poet. Just how good
    a poem should be
Before one releases it, either into one's own work or
    then into the purview of others,
May be decided by applying the following rules: ask 1) Is
    it astonishing?
Am I pleased each time I read it? Does it say something
    I was unaware of
Before I sat down to write it? and 2) Do I stand up from
    it a better man
Or a wiser, or both? or can the two not be separated?
    3) Is it really by me
Or have I stolen it from somewhere else? (This some-
    times happens,
Though it is comparatively rare.) 4) Does it reveal some-
    thing about me
I never want anyone to know? 5) Is it sufficiently
    "modern"?
(More about this a little later) 6) Is it in my own "voice"?

Along with, of course, the more obvious questions,
    such as
7) Is there any unwanted awkwardness, cheap effects,
    asking illegitimately for attention,
Show-offiness, cuteness, pseudo-profundity, old hat
    checks,
Unassimilated dream fragments, or other "literary,"
    "kiss-me-I'm-poetical" junk?
Is my poem free of this? 8) Does it move smoothly and
    swiftly
From excitement to dream and then come flooding
    reason
With purity and soundness and joy? 9) Is this the kind of
    poem
I would envy in another if he could write? 10)
Would I be happy to go to Heaven with this pinned on
    to my
Angelic jacket as an entrance show? Oh, would I? And if
    you can answer to all these Yes
Except for the 4th one, to which the answer should
    be No,
Then you can release it, at least for the time being.
I would look at it again, though, perhaps in two hours,
    then after one or two weeks,
And then a month later, at which time you can probably
    be sure.

To look at a poem again of course causes anxiety
In many cases, but that pain a writer must learn to
    endure,
For without it he will be like a chicken which never
    knows what it is doing

And goes feathering and fluttering through life. When
    one finds the poem
Inadequate, then one must revise, and this can be very
    hard going
Indeed. For the original "inspiration" is not there. Some
    poets never master the
Art of doing this, and remain "minor" or almost nothing
    at all.
Such have my sympathy but not my praise. My sympa-
    thy because
Such work is difficult, and most persons accomplish
    nothing whatsoever
In the course of their lives; at least these poets are writing
"First versions," but they can never win the praise
Of a discerning reader until they take hard-hearted
    Revision to bed
And win her to their cause and create through her
    "second-time-around" poems
Or even "third-time-around" ones. There are several
    ways to gain
The favors of this lady. One is unstinting labor, but be
    careful
You do not ruin what is already there by unfeeling
    rewriting
That makes it more "logical" but cuts out its heart.
Sometimes neglecting a poem for several weeks is best,
As if you had forgotten you wrote it, and changing it then
As swiftly as you can—in that way, you will avoid at least
    dry "re-detailing"
Which is fatal to any art. Sometimes the confidence you
    have from a successful poem

Can help you to find for another one the changes you
    want.
Actually, a night's sleep and a new day filled with confi-
    dence are very desirable,
And, once you get used to the ordinary pains that go
    with revising,
You may grow to like it very much. It gives one the
    strange feeling
That one is "working on" something, as an engineer
    does, or a pilot
When something goes wrong with the plane; whereas
    the inspired first version of a poem
Is more like simply a lightning flash to the heart.
Revising gives one the feeling of being a builder. And if
    it brings pain? Well,
It sometimes does, and women have pain giving birth to
    children
Yet often wish to do so again, and perhaps the grizzly
    bear has pain
Burrowing down into the ground to sleep all winter. In
    writing
The pain is relatively minor. We need not speak of it
    again
Except in the case of the fear that one has "lost one's
    talent,"
Which I will go into immediately. This fear
Is a perfectly logical fear for poets to have,
And all of them, from time to time, have it. It is very rare
For what one does best and that on which one's happi-
    ness depends
To so large an extent, to be itself dependent on factors

Seemingly beyond one's control. For whence cometh
    Inspiration?
Will she stay in her Bower of Bliss or come to me this
    evening?
Have I gotten too old for her kisses? Will she like that
    boy there rather than me?
Am I a dried-up old hog? Is this then the end of it?
    Haven't I
Lost that sweet easy knack I had last week,
Last month, last year, last decade, which pleased everyone
And especially pleased me? I no longer can feel the
    warmth of it—
Oh, I have indeed lost it! Etcetera. And when you write
    a new poem
You like, you forget this anguish, and so on till your
    death,
Which you'll be remembered beyond, not for "keeping
    your talent,"
But for what you wrote, in spite of your worries and fears.

The truth is, I think, that one does not lose one's talent,
Although one can misplace it—in attempts to remain in
    the past,
In profitless ventures intended to please those whom
Could one see them clearly one would not wish to
    please,
In opera librettos, or even in one's life
Somewhere. But you can almost always find it, perhaps
    in trying new forms
Or not in form at all but in the (seeming) lack of it—
Write "stream of consciousness." Or, differently again,
    do some translations.

Renounce repeating the successes of the years before.
   Seek
A success of a type undreamed of. Write a poetic fishing
   manual. Try an Art of Love.
Whatever, be on the lookout for what you feared you
   had lost,
The talent you misplaced. The only ways really to lose it
Are serious damage to the brain and being so attracted
To something else (such as money, sex, repairing expen-
   sive engines)
That you forget it completely. In that case, how care
   that it is lost?
In spite of the truth of all this, however, I am aware
That fear of lost talent is a natural part of a poet's
   existence.
So be prepared for it, and do not let it get you down.

Just how much experience a poet should have
To be sure he has enough to be sure he is an adequate
   knower
And feeler and thinker of experience as it exists in our
   time
Is a tough one to answer, and the only sure rule I can
   think of
Is experience as much as you can and write as much as
   you can.
These two can be contradictory. A great many experi-
   ences are worthless
At least as far as poetry is concerned. Whereas the least
   promising,
Seemingly, will throw a whole epic in one's lap.
   However, that is Sarajevo

And not cause. Probably. I do not know what to tell you
That would apply to all cases. I would suggest travel
And learning at least one other language (five or six
Could be a distraction). As for sexuality and other
Sensual pleasures, you must work that out for yourself.
You should know the world, men, women, space, wind,
    islands, governments,
The history of art, news of the lost continents, plants,
    evenings,
Mornings, days. But you must also have time to write.
You need environments for your poems and also people,
But you also need life, you need to care about these
    things
And these persons, and that is the difficulty, that
What you will find best to write about cannot be
    experienced
Merely as "material." There are some arts one picks up
Of "living sideways," and forwards and backwards at the
    same time,
But they often do not work—or do, to one's disadvantage:
You feel, "I did not experience that. That cow did
More than I. Or that 'Blue Man' without a thought in
    the world
Beyond existing. He is the one who really exists.
That is true poetry. I am nothing." I suggest waiting a
    few hours
Before coming to such a rash decision and going off
Riding on a camel yourself. For you cannot escape your
    mind
And your strange interest in writing poetry, which will
    make you,
Necessarily, an experiencer and un-experiencer

Of life, at the same time, but you should realize that
    what you do
Is immensely valuable, and difficult, too, in a way riding
    a camel is not,
Though that is valuable too—you two will amaze each
    other,
The Blue Man and you, and that is also a part of life
Which you must catch in your poem. As for how much
    one's poetry
Should "reflect one's experience," I do not think it can
    avoid
Doing that. The naïve version of such a concern
Of course is stupid, but if you feel the need to "confront"
Something, try it, and see how it goes. To "really find
    your emotions,"
Write, and keep working at it. Success in the literary
    world
Is mostly irrelevant but may please you. It is good to
    have a friend
To help you past the monsters on the way. Becoming
    famous will not hurt you
Unless you are foolishly overcaptivated and forget
That this too is merely a part of your "experience." For
    those who make poets famous
In general know nothing about poetry. Remember your
    obligation is to write,
And, in writing, to be serious without being solemn,
    fresh without being cold,
To be inclusive without being asinine, particular
Without being picky, feminine without being effeminate,
Masculine without being brutish, human while keeping
    all the animal graces

You had inside the womb, and beast-like without being
   inhuman.
Let your language be delectable always, and fresh and
   true.
Don't be conceited. Let your compassion guide you
And your excitement. And always bring your endeavors
   to their end.

One thing a poem needs is to be complete
In itself and not need others to complement it.
Therefore this poem about writing should be complete
With information about everything concerned in the act
Of creating a poem. A work also should not be too long.
Each line should give a gathered new sensation
Of "Oh, now I know that, and want to go on!"
"Measure," which decides how long a poem should be,
Is difficult, because possible elaboration is endless,
As endless as the desire to write, so the decision to end
A poem is generally arbitrary yet must be made
Except in the following two cases: when one embarks on
   an epic
Confident that it will last all one's life,
Or when one deliberately continues it past hope of
   concluding—
Edmund Spenser and Ezra Pound seem examples
Of one of these cases or the other. And no one knows
   how
The Faerie Queene continued (if it did, as one writer said,
The last parts destroyed in the sacking of Spenser's
   house
By the crazed but justified Irish, or was it by his
   servants?).

It may be that Spenser never went beyond Book Six
In any serious way, because the thought of ending was
        unpleasant,
Yet his plan for the book, if he wrote on, would oblige
        him to end it. This unlike Pound
Who had no set determined place to cease. Coming to a
        stop
And giving determined form is easiest in drama,
It may be, or in short songs, like "We'll Go
No More a-Roving," one of Byron's most
Touching poems, an absolute success, the best
Short one, I believe, that Byron wrote. In all these
Cases, then, except for "lifetime" poems, there is a point
        one reaches
When one knows that one must come to an end,
And that is the point that must be reached. To reach it,
        however,
One may have to cut out much of what one has written
        along the way,
For the end does not necessarily come of itself
But must be coaxed forth from the material, like a
        blossom.

Anyone who would like to write an epic poem
May wish to have a plot in mind, or at least a mood—the
Minimum requirement is a form. Sometimes a stanza,
Like Spenser's, or Ariosto's ottava rima, will set the
        poem going
Downhill and uphill and all around experience
And the world in the maddest way imaginable. Enough,
In this case, to begin, and to let oneself be carried

By the wind of eight (or, in the case of Spenser, nine)
    loud rhymes.
Sometimes blank verse will tempt the amateur
Of endless writing; sometimes a couplet; sometimes
    "free verse."
"Skeltonics" are hard to sustain over an extended period
As are, in English, and in Greek for all I know,
    "Sapphics."
The epic has a clear advantage over any sort of lyric
Poem in being there when you go back to it to continue.
    The
Lyric is fleeting, usually caught in one
Breath or not at all (though see what has been said before
About revision—it can be done). The epic one is
    writing, however,
Like a great sheep dog is always there
Wagging and waiting to welcome one into the corner
To be petted and sent forth to fetch a narrative bone.
Oh writing an epic! what a pleasure you are
And what an agony! But the pleasure is greater than the
    agony,
And the achievement is the sweetest thing of all. Men
    raise the problem,
"How can one write an epic in the modern world?" One
    can answer,
"Look around you—tell me how one cannot!" Which is
    more or less what
Juvenal said about Satire, but epic is a form
Our international time-space plan cries out for—or so it
    seems
To one observer. The lyric is a necessity too,

And those you may write either alone
Or in the interstices of your epic poem, like flowers
Crannied in the Great Wall of China as it sweeps across
    the earth.
To write only lyrics is to be sad, perhaps,
Or fidgety, or overexcited, too dependent on
    circumstance—
But there is a way out of that. The lyric must be bent
Into a more operative form, so that
Fragments of being reflect absolutes (see for example the
    verse of
Williarn Carlos Williams or Frank O'Hara), and you
    can go on
Without saying it all every time. If you can master the
    knack of it,
You are a fortunate poet, and a skilled one. You should
    read
A great deal, and be thinking of writing poetry all the
    time.
Total absorption in poetry is one of the finest things in
    existence—
It should not make you feel guilty. Everyone is absorbed
    in something.
The sailor is absorbed in the sea. Poetry is the mediation
    of life.
The epic is particularly appropriate to our contemporary
    world
Because we are so uncertain of everything and also know
    too much,
A curious and seemingly contradictory condition, which
    the epic salves

By giving us our knowledge and our grasp, with all our
        lack of control as well.
The lyric adjusts to us like a butterfly, then epically
        eludes our grasp.
Poetic drama in our time seems impossible but actually
        exists as
A fabulous possibility just within our reach. To write
        drama
One must conceive of an answerer to what one says, as I
        am now conceiving of you.

As to whether or not you use rhyme and how "modern"
        you are
It is something your genius can decide on every morning
When you get out of bed. What a clear day! Good luck
        at it!
Though meter is probably, and rhyme too, probably,
        dead
For a while, except in narrative stanzas. You try it out.
The pleasure of the easy inflection between meter and
        these easy vocable lines
Is a pleasure, if you are able to have it, you are unlikely
        to renounce.
As for "surrealistic" methods and techniques, they have
        become a
Natural part of writing. Your poetry, if possible, should
        be extended
Somewhat beyond your experience, while still remaining
        true to it;
Unconscious material should play a luscious part
In what you write, since without the unconscious part

You know very little; and your plainest statements
        should be
Even better than plain. A reader should put your work
        down puzzled,
Distressed, and illuminated, ready to believe
It is curious to be alive. As for your sense of what good
        you
Do by writing, compared to what good statesmen,
        doctors,
Flower salesmen, and missionaries do, perhaps you do
        less
And perhaps more. If you would like to try one of these
Other occupations for a while, try it. I imagine you will
        find
That poetry does something they do not do, whether it is
More important or not, and if you like poetry, you will
        like doing that yourself.

Poetry need not be an exclusive occupation.
Some think it should, some think it should not. But you
        should
Have years for poetry, or at least if not years months
At certain points in your life. Weeks, days, and hours
        may not suffice.
Almost any amount of time suffices to be a "minor poet"
Once you have mastered a certain amount of the craft
For writing a poem, but I do not see the good of minor
        poetry,
Like going to the Tour d'Argent to get dinner for your
        dog,
Or "almost" being friends with someone, or hanging
        around but not attending a school,

Or being a nurse's aid for the rest of your life after
    getting a degree in medicine,
What is the point of it? And some may wish to write
    songs
And use their talent that way. Others may even end up
    writing ads.
To those of you who are left, when these others have
    departed,
And you are a strange bunch, I alone address these
    words.

It is true that good poetry is difficult to write.
Poetry is an escape from anxiety and a source of it as
    well.
On the whole, it seems to me worthwhile. At the end of
    a poem
One may be tempted to grow too universal,
    philosophical, and vague
Or to bring in History, or the Sea, but one should not
    do that
If one can possibly help it, since it makes
Each thing one writes sound like everything else,
And poetry and life are not like that. Now I have said
    enough.

The Boiling Water

A serious moment for the water is when it boils
And though one usually regards it merely as a
    convenience

To have the boiling water available for bath or table
Occasionally there is someone around who understands
The importance of this moment for the water—maybe a
    saint,
Maybe a poet, maybe a crazy man, or just someone tem-
    porarily disturbed
With his mind "floating," in a sense, away from his
    deepest
Personal concerns to more "unreal" things. A lot of
    poetry
Can come from perceptions of this kind, as well as a lot
    of insane conversations.
Intense people can sometimes get stuck on topics like
    these
And keep you far into the night with them. Still, it is true
That the water has just started to boil. How important
For the water! And now I see that the tree is waving in
    the wind
(I assume it is the wind)—at least, its branches are. In
    order to see
Hidden meanings, one may have to ignore
The most exciting ones, those that are most directly
    appealing
And yet it is only these appealing ones that, often, one
    can trust
To make one's art solid and true, just as it is sexual
    attraction
One has to trust, often, in love. So the boiling water's
    seriousness
Is likely to go unobserved until the exact strange
    moment
(And what a temptation it is to end the poem here

With some secret thrust) when it involuntarily comes
    into the mind
And then one can write of it. A serious moment for this
    poem will be when it ends,
It will be like the water's boiling, that for which we've
    waited
Without trying to think of it too much, since "a watched
    pot never boils,"
And a poem with its ending figured out is difficult to
    write.

Once the water is boiling, the heater has a choice: to
    look at it
And let it boil and go on seeing what it does, or to take it
    off and use the water for tea,
Chocolate or coffee or beef consommé. You don't drink
    the product then
Until the water has ceased to boil, for otherwise
It would burn your tongue. Even hot water is dangerous
    and has a thorn
Like the rose, or a horn like the baby ram. Modest hot
    water, and the tree
Blowing in the wind. The connection here is how
    serious is it for the tree
To have its arms wave (its branches)? How did it ever get
    such flexibility
In the first place? and who put the boiling potentiality
    into water?
A tree will not boil, nor will the wind. Think of the
    dinners
We could have, and the lunches, and the dreams, if only
    they did.

But that is not to think of what things are really about.
    For the tree
I don't know how serious it is to be waving, though water's
    boiling
Is more dramatic, is more like a storm, high tide
And the ship goes down, but it comes back up as coffee,
    chocolate, or tea.

How many people I have drunk tea or coffee with
And thought about the boiling water hardly at all, just
    waiting for it to boil
So there could be coffee or chocolate or tea. And then
    what?
The body stimulated, the brain alarmed, grounds in the
    pot,
The tree, waving, out the window, perhaps with a little
    more élan
Because we saw it that way, because the water boiled,
    because we drank tea.

The water boils almost every time the same old way
And still it is serious, because it is boiling. That is what,
I think, one should see. From this may come compassion,
Compassion and a knowledge of nature, although most
    of the time
I know I am not going to think about it. It would be crazy
To give such things precedence over such affairs of one's
    life
As involve more fundamental satisfactions. But is going
    to the beach
More fundamental than seeing the water boil? Saving of
    money,

It's well known, can result from an aesthetic attitude,
      since a rock
Picked up in the street contains all the shape and hard-
      ness of the world.
One sidewalk leads everywhere. You don't have to be in
      Estapan.

A serious moment for the island is when its trees
Begin to give it shade, and another is when the ocean
      washes
Big heavy things against its side. One walks around and
      looks at the island
But not really at it, at what is on it, and one thinks,
It must be serious, even, to be this island, at all, here,
Since it is lying here exposed to the whole sea. All its
Moments might be serious. It is serious, in such windy
      weather, to be a sail
Or an open window, or a feather flying in the street.
Seriousness, how often I have thought of seriousness
And how little I have understood it, except this: serious
      is urgent
And it has to do with change. You say to the water,
It's not necessary to boil now, and you turn it off. It stops
Fidgeting. And starts to cool. You put your hand in it
And say, The water isn't serious any more. It has the
      potential,
However—that urgency to give off bubbles, to
Change itself to steam. And the wind,
When it becomes part of a hurricane, blowing up the
      beach
And the sand dunes can't keep it away.

Fainting is one sign of seriousness, crying is another.
Shuddering all over is another one.

A serious moment for the telephone is when it rings,
And a person answers, it is Angelica, or is it you
And finally, at last, who answer, my wing, my past, my
Angel, my flume, and my de-control, my orange and my
        good-bye kiss,
My extravagance, and my weight at fifteen years old
And at the height of my intelligence, oh Cordillera two
And sandals one, C'est toi à l'appareil? Is that you at
The telephone, and when it snows, a serious moment for
        the bus is when it snows
For then it has to slow down for sliding, and every
        moment is a trust.

A serious moment for the fly is when its wings
Are moving, and a serious moment for the duck
Is when it swims, when it first touches water, then spreads
Its smile upon the water, its feet begin to paddle, it is in
And above the water, pushing itself forward, a duck.
And a serious moment for the sky is when, completely
        blue,
It feels some clouds coming; another when it turns dark.
A serious moment for the match is when it bursts into
        flame
And is all alone, living, in that instant, that beautiful
        second for which it was made.
So much went into it! The men at the match factory, the
        mood of
The public, the sand covering the barn

So it was hard to find the phosphorus, and now this
    flame,
This pink white ecstatic light blue! For the telephone
    when it rings,
For the wind when it blows, and for the match when it
    bursts into flame.

Serious, all our life is serious, and we see around us
Seriousness for other things, that touches us and seems
    as if it might be giving clues.
The seriousness of the house when it is being built
And is almost completed, and then the moment when it
    is completed.
The seriousness of the bee when it stings. We say, He
    has taken his life,
Merely to sting. Why would he do that? And we feel
We aren't concentrated enough, not pure, not deep
As the buzzing bee. The bee flies into the house
And lights on a chair arm and sits there, waiting for
    something to be
Other than it is, so he can fly again. He is boiling,
    waiting. Soon he is forgotten
And everyone is speaking again.

Seriousness, everyone speaks of seriousness
Certain he knows or seeking to know what it is. A child
    is bitten by an animal
And that is serious. The doctor has a serious life. He is
    somewhat, in that, like the bee.
And water! water—how it is needed! and it is always
    going down

Seeking its own level, evaporating, boiling, now
    changing into ice
And snow, now making up our bodies. We drink the
    coffee
And somewhere in this moment is the chance
We will never see each other again. It is serious for the
    tree
To be moving, the flexibility of its moving
Being the sign of its continuing life. And now there are
    its blossoms
And the fact that it is blossoming again, it is filling up with
Pink and whitish blossoms, it is full of them, the wind
    blows, it is
Warm, though, so much is happening, it is spring, the
    people step out
And doors swing in, and billions of insects are born. You
    call me and tell me
You feel that your life is not worth living. I say I will
    come to see you. I put the key in
And the car begins to clatter, and now it starts.

Serious for me that I met you, and serious for you
That you met me, and that we do not know
If we will ever be close to anyone again. Serious the
    recognition of the probability
That we will, although time stretches terribly in be-
    tween. It is serious not to know
And to know and to try to figure things out. One's legs
Cross, foot swings, and a cigarette is blooming, a gray
    bouquet, and
The water is boiling. Serious the birth (what a phenom-
    enon!) of anything and

The movements of the trees, and for the lovers
Everything they do and see. Serious intermittently for
	consciousness
The sign that something may be happening, always,
	today,
That is enough. For the germ when it enters or leaves a
	body. For the fly when it lifts its little wings.

To Marina

So many convolutions and not enough simplicity!
When I had you to write to it
Was different. The quiet, dry Z
Leaped up to the front of the alphabet.
You sit, stilling your spoons
With one hand; you move them with the other.
Radio says, "God is a postmaster."
You said, Ziss is lawflee. And in the heat
Of writing to you I wrote simply. I thought
These are the best things I shall ever write
And have ever written. I thought of nothing but
	touching you.
Thought of seeing you and, in a separate thought, of
	looking at you.
You were concentrated feeling and thought.
You were like the ocean
In which my poems were the swimming. I brought you
Ear rings. You said, These are lawflee. We went

To some beach, where the sand was dirty. Just going in
To the bathing house with you drove me "out of my
        mind."

It is wise to be witty. The shirt collar's far away.
Men tramp up and down the city on this windy day.
I am feeling a-political as a shell
Brought off some fish. Twenty-one years
Ago I saw you and loved you still.
Still! It wasn't plenty
Of time. Read Anatole France. Bored, a little. Read
Tolstoy, replaced and overcome. You read Stendhal.
I told you to. Where was replacement
Then? I don't know. He shushed us back into ourselves.
I used to understand
The highest excitement. Someone died
And you were distant. I went away
And made you distant. Where are you now? I see the
        chair
And hang onto it for sustenance. Good God how you
        kissed me
And I held you. You screamed
And I wasn't bothered by anything. Was nearest you.

And you were so realistic
Preferring the Soviet Bookstore
To my literary dreams.
"You don't like war," you said
After reading a poem
In which I'd simply said I hated war
In a whole list of things. To you
It seemed a position, to me

It was all a flux, especially then.
I was in an
Unexpected situation.
Let's take a walk
I wrote. And I love you as a sheriff
Searches for a walnut. And And so unless
I'm going to see your face
Bien soon, and you said
You must take me away, and
Oh Kenneth
You like everything
To be pleasant. I was burning
Like an arch
Made out of trees.

I'm not sure we ever actually took a walk.
We were so damned nervous. I was heading somewhere.
        And you had to be
At an appointment, or else be found out! Illicit love!
It's not a thing to think of. Nor is it when it's licit!
It is too much! And it wasn't enough. The achievement
I thought I saw possible when I loved you
Was that really achievement? Were you my
Last chance to feel that I had lost my chance?
I grew faint at your voice on the telephone
Electricity and all colors were mine, and the tops of hills
And everything that breathes. That was a feeling. Certain
Artistic careers had not even started. And I
Could have surpassed them. I could have I think put the
Whole world under our feet. You were in the restau-
        rant. It

Was Chinese. We have walked three blocks. Or four
        blocks. It is New York
In nineteen fifty-three. Nothing has as yet happened
That will ever happen and will mean as much to me. You
        smile, and turn your head.
What rocketing there was in my face and in my head
And bombing everywhere in my body
I loved you I knew suddenly
That nothing had meant anything like you
I must have hoped (crazily) that something would
As if thinking you were the person I had become.

My sleep is beginning to be begun. And the sheets were
        on the bed.
A clock rang a bird's song rattled into my typewriter.
I had been thinking about songs which were very
        abstract.
Language was the champion. The papers lay piled on
        my desk
It was really a table. Now, the telephone. Hello, what?
What is my life like now? Engaged, studying and
        looking around
The library, teaching—I took it rather easy
A little too easy—we went to the ballet
Then dark becomes the light (blinding) of the next
        eighty days
Orchestra cup became As beautiful as an orchestra or a
        cup, and
Locked climbs becomes If we were locked, well not
        quite, rather

Oh penniless could I really die, and I understood
    everything
Which before was running this way and that in my head
I saw titles, volumes, and suns I felt the hot
Pressure of your hands in that restaurant
To which, along with glasses, plates, lamps, lusters,
Tablecloths, napkins, and all the other junk
You added my life for it was entirely in your hands
    then—
My life
Yours, My Sister Life of Pasternak's beautiful title
My life without a life, my life in a life, my life impure
And my life pure, life seen as an entity
One death and a variety of days
And only one life.

I wasn't ready
For you.

I understood nothing
Seemingly except my feelings
You were whirling
In your life
I was keeping
Everything in my head
An artist friend's apartment
Five flights up the
Lower East Side nineteen
Fifty-something I don't know
What we made love the first time I
Almost died I had never felt

That way it was like being stamped on in Hell
It was roses of Heaven
My friends seemed turned to me to empty shell

On the railroad train's red velvet back
You put your hand in mime and said
"I told him"
Or was it the time after that?
I said Why did you
Do that you said I thought
It was over. Why? Because you were so
Nervous of my being there it was something I thought

I read
Tolstoy. You said
I don't like the way it turns out (*Anna
Karenina*) I had just liked the strength
Of the feeling you thought
About the end. I wanted
To I don't know what never leave you
Five flights up the June
Street emptied of fans, cups, kites, cops, eats, nights, no
The night was there
And something like air I love you Marina
Eighty-five days
Four thousand three hundred and sixty-
Two minutes all poetry was changed
For me what did I do in exchange
I am selfish, afraid you are
Overwhelmingly parade, back, sunshine, dreams
Later thousands of dreams

You said
You make me feel nawble (noble). I said
Yes. I said
To nothingness, This is all poems. Another one said
        (later)
That is so American. You were Russian.
You thought of your feelings, one said, not of her,
Not of the real situation. But my feelings were a part,
They were the force of the real situation. Truer to say I
        thought
Not of the whole situation
For your husband was also a part
And your feelings about your child were a part
And all my other feelings were a part. We
Turned this way and that, up-
Stairs then down
Into the streets.
Did I die because I didn't stay with you?
Or what did I lose of my life? I lost
You. I put you
In everything I wrote.

I used that precious material I put it in forms
Also I wanted to break down the forms
Poetry was a real occupation
To hell with the norms, with what is already written
Twenty-nine in love finds pure expression
Twenty-nine years you my whole life's digression
Not taken and Oh Kenneth
Everything afterwards seemed nowhere near
What I could do then in several minutes—
I wrote,

"I want to look at you all day long
Because you are mine."

I am twenty-nine, pocket flap folded
And I am smiling I am looking out at a world that
I significantly re-created from inside
Out of contradictory actions and emotions. I look like a
    silly child that
Photograph that year—big glasses, unthought-of
    clothes,
A suit, slight mess in general, cropped hair. And some-
    one liked me,
Loved me a lot, I think. And someone else had, you had,
    too. I was
Undrenched by the tears I'd shed later about this whole
    thing when
I'd telephone you I'd be all nerves, though in fact
All life was a factor and all my nerves were in my head. I
    feel
Peculiar. Or I feel nothing. I am thinking about this
    poem. I am thinking about your raincoat,
I am worried about the tactfulness,
About the truth of what I say.
I am thinking about my standards for my actions
About what they were
You raised my standards for harmony and for happiness
    so much
And, too, the sense of a center
Which did amazing things for my taste
But my taste for action? for honesty, for directness in
    behavior?

I believe I simply never felt that anything could go wrong
This was abject stupidity
I also was careless in how I drove then and in what I ate
And drank it was easier to feel that nothing could go
     wrong
I had those feelings. I
Did not those things. I was involved in such and such
A situation, artistically and socially. We never spent a
     night
Together it is the New York of
Aquamarine sunshine and the Loew's Theater's blazing
     swing of light
In the middle of the day

Let's take a walk
Into the world
Where if our shoes get white
With snow, is it snow, Marina,
Is it snow or light?
Let's take a walk

Every detail is everything in its place (Aristotle). Litera-
     ture is a cup
And we are the malted. The time is a glass. A June bug
     comes
And a carpenter spits on a plane, the flowers ruffle ear
     rings.
I am so dumb-looking. And you are so beautiful.

Sitting in the Hudson Tube
Walking up the fusky street
Always waiting to see you

You the original creation of all my You, you the you
In every poem the hidden one whom I am talking to
Worked at Bamberger's once I went with you to Cerutti's
Bar—on Madison Avenue? I held your hand and you said
Kenneth you are playing with fire. I said
Something witty in reply.
It was the time of the McCarthy trial
Hot sunlight on lunches. You squirted
Red wine into my mouth.
My feelings were like a fire my words became very clear
My psyche or whatever it is that puts together motions
    and emotions
Was unprepared. There was a good part
And an alarmingly bad part which didn't correspond—
No letters! no seeming connection! your slim pale hand
It actually was, your blondness and your turning-
    around-to-me look. Good-bye Kenneth.

No, Marina, don't go
And what had been before would come after
Not to be mysterious we'd be together make love again
It was the wildest thing I've done
I can hardly remember it
It has gotten by now
So mixed up with losing you
The two almost seem in some way the same. You
Wore something soft—angora? cashmere?
I remember that it was black. You turned around
And on such a spring day which went on and on and on
I actually think I felt that I could keep
The strongest of all feelings contained inside me
Producing endless emotional designs.

With the incomparable feeling of rising and of being
     like a banner
Twenty seconds worth twenty-five years
With feeling noble extremely mobile and very free
With Taking a Walk With You, West Wind, In Love
     With You, and Yellow Roses
With pleasure I felt my leg muscles and my brain couldn't
     hold
With the Empire State Building the restaurant your
     wrist bones with Greenwich Avenue
In nineteen fifty-one with heat humidity a dog pissing
     with neon
With the feeling that at last
My body had something to do and so did my mind

You sit
At the window. You call
Me, across Paris,
Amsterdam, New
York. Kenneth!
My Soviet
Girlhood. My
Spring, summer
And fall. Do you
Know you have
Missed some of them?
Almost all. I am
Waiting and I
Am fading I
Am fainting I'm
In a degrading state
Of inactivity. A ball

Rolls in the gutter. I have
Two hands to
Stop it. I am
A flower I pick
The vendor his
Clothes getting up
Too early and
What is it makes this rose
Into what is more fragrant than what is not?

I am stunned I am feeling tortured
By "A man of words and not a man of deeds"

I was waiting in a taxicab
It was white letters in white paints it was you
Spring comes, summer, then fall
And winter. We really have missed
All of that, whatever else there was
In those years so sanded by our absence.
I never saw you for as long as half a day

You were crying outside the bus station
And I was crying—
I knew that this really was my life—
I kept thinking of how we were crying
Later, when I was speaking, driving, walking,
Looking at doorways and colors, mysterious entrances
Sometimes I'd be pierced as by a needle
Sometimes be feverish as from a word
Books closed and I'd think
I can't read this book, I threw away my life
These held on to their lives. I was

Excited by praise from anyone, startled by criticism,
    always hating it
Traveling around Europe and being excited
It was all in reference to you
And feeling I was not gradually forgetting
What your temples and cheekbones looked like
And always with this secret

Later I thought
That what I had done was reasonable
It may have been reasonable
I also thought that I saw what had appealed to me
So much about you, the way you responded
To everything your excitement about
Me, I had never seen that. And the fact
That you were Russian, very mysterious, all that I didn't
    know
About you—and you didn't know
Me, for I was as strange to you as you were to me.
You were like my first trip to France you had
Made no assumptions. I could be
Clearly and passionately and
Nobly (as you'd said) who I was—at the outer limits of
    my life
Of my life as my life could be
Ideally. But what about the dark part all this lifted
Me out of? Would my bad moods, my uncertainties, my
Distrust of people I was close to, the
Twisty parts of my ambition, my
Envy, all have gone away? And if
They hadn't gone, what? For didn't I need

All the strength you made me feel I had, to deal
With the difficulties of really having you?
Where could we have been? But I saw so many new
    possibilities
That it made me rather hate reality
Or I think perhaps I already did
I didn't care about the consequences
Because they weren't "poetic" weren't "ideal"

And oh well you said we walk along
Your white dress your blue dress your green
Blouse with sleeves then one without
Sleeves and we are speaking
Of things but not of very much because underneath it
I am raving I am boiling I am afraid
You ask me Kenneth what are you thinking
If I could say
It all then I thought if I could say
Exactly everything and have it still be as beautiful
Billowing over, riding over both our doubts
Some kind of perfection and what did I actually
Say? Marina it's late. Marina
It's early. I love you. Or else, What's this street?
You were the perfection of my life
And I couldn't have you. That is, I didn't.
I couldn't think. I wrote, instead. I would have had
To think hard, to figure everything out
About how I could be with you,
Really, which I couldn't do
In those moments of permanence we had
As we walked along.

We walk through the park in the sun. It is the end.
You phone me. I send you a telegram. It
Is the end. I keep
Thinking about you, grieving about you. It is the end. I
    write
Poems about you, to you. They
Are no longer simple. No longer
Are you there to see every day or
Every other or every third or fourth warm day
And now it has been twenty-five years
But those feelings kept orchestrating I mean rehearsing
Rehearsing in me and tuning up
While I was doing a thousand other things, the band
Is ready, I am over fifty years old and there's no you—
And no me, either, not as I was then,
When it was the Renaissance
Filtered through my nerves and weakness
Of nineteen fifty-four or fifty-three,
When I had you to write to, when I could see you
And it could change.

Days and Nights

1. The Invention of Poetry

It came to me that all this time
There had been no real poetry and that it needed to be
    invented.
Some recommended discovering

What was already there. Others,
Taking a view from further up the hill (remnant
Of old poetry), said just go and start wherever you are.

It was not the kind of line
I wanted so I crossed it out
"Today I don't think I'm very inspired"—
What an existence! How hard to concentrate
On what is the best kind of existence!
What's sure is having only one existence
And its already having a shape.

Extase de mes vingt ans—
French girl with pure gold eyes
In which shine internal rhyme and new kinds of stanzas

When I said to F, Why do you write poems?
He said, Look at most of the poems
That have already been written!

All alone writing
And lacking self-confidence
And in another way filled with self-confidence
And in another way devoted to the brick wall
As a flower is when hummed on by a bee

I thought This is the one I am supposed to like best
The totally indifferent one
Who simply loves and identifies himself with something
Or someone and cares not what others think nor of time
The one who identifies himself with a wall.

I didn't think I was crazy
I thought Orpheus chasms trireme hunch coats melody
And then No that isn't good enough

I wrote poems on the edges of the thistles
Which my walking companions couldn't understand
But that's when I was a baby compared to now

"That is so much like you and your poetry."
This puts me in a self-congratulatory mood
Which I want to "feel out," so we sit together and talk
All through the winter afternoon.

I smoked
After writing five or ten lines
To enjoy what I had already written
And to not have to write any more

I stop smoking
Until after lunch
It is morning
It is spring
The day is breaking
Ten—eleven—noon
I am not smoking
I am asleep

Sense of what primitive man is, in cave and with
        primitive life
Comes over me one bright morning as I lie in bed
Whoosh! to the typewriter. Lunch! And I go down.

What have I lost?
The Coleridge joke, as W would say.

William Carlos Williams, I wrote
As the end word of a sestina. And *grass*
Sleep, *hog snout*, *breath*, and *dream*.
I never finished it.

I come down the hill—cloud
I like living on a hill—head
You are so lucky to be alive—jokes
It chimes at every moment—stung

So much of it was beyond me
The winding of the national highway
The fragments of glass in the convent wall
To say nothing of the habits of the bourgeoisie
And all those pleasures, the neat coat,
The bought wine, and the enabling of the
        pronouncements

For Christ's sake you're missing the whole day
Cried someone and I said Shut up
I want to sleep and what he accomplished in the hours I
        slept
I do not know and what I accomplished in my sleep
Was absolutely nothing

How much is in the poet and how much in the poem?
You can't get to the one but he gives you the other.
Is he holding back? No, but his experience is like a
        bubble.

When he gives it to you, it breaks. Those left-over soap
    dots are the work.

Oh you've done plenty I said when he was feeling
    despondent
Look at X and L and M. But they don't do anything, he
    replied.

At the window I could see
What never could be inside me
Since I was twelve: pure being
Without desire for the other, not even for the necktie or
    the dog

2. The Stones of Time

The bathtub is white and full of strips
And stripes of red and blue and green and white
Where the painter has taken a bath! Now comes the poet
Wrapped in a huge white towel, with his head full of
    imagery.

Try being really attentive to your life
Instead of to your writing for a change once in a while

Sometimes one day one hour one minute oh I've done that
What happened? I got married and was in a good mood

We wrote so much that we thought it couldn't be any
    good
Till we read it over and then thought how amazing it was!

Athena gave Popeye a Butterfinger filled with stars
Is the kind of poetry Z and I used to stuff in jars

When we took a walk he was afraid
Of the dogs who came in parade
To sniffle at the feet
Of two of the greatest poets of the age.

The stars came out
And I was still writing
My God where's dinner
Here's dinner
My wife! I love you

Do you remember in Paris
When I was thinner
And the sun came through the shutters like a knife

I said to so many people once, "I write poetry."
They said, "Oh, so you are a poet." Or they said,
"What kind of poetry do you write? modern poetry?"
Or "My brother-in-law is a poet also."
Now if I say, "I am the poet Kenneth Koch," they say "I
        think I've heard of you"
Or "I'm sorry but that doesn't ring a bell" or
"Would you please move out of the way? You're
        blocking my view
Of that enormous piece of meat that they are lowering
        into the Bay
Of Pigs." What? Or "What kind of poetry do you write?"

"Taste," I said to J and he said
"What else is there?" but he was looking around.

"All the same, she isn't made like that,"
Marguerite said, upon meeting Janice,
To her husband Eddie, and since
Janice was pregnant this had a clear meaning
Like the poetry of Robert Burns.

You must learn to write in form first, said the dumb poet.
After several years of that you can write in free verse.
But of course no verse is really "free," said the dumb poet.
Thank you, I said. It's been great talking to you!

Sweet are the uses of adversity
Became Sweetheart cabooses of diversity
And Sweet art cow papooses at the university
And sea bar Calpurnia flower havens' re-noosed knees

A book came out, and then another book
Which was unlike the first,
Which was unlike the love
And the nightmares and the fisticuffs that inspired it
And the other poets, with their egos and their works,
Which I sometimes read reluctantly and sometimes with
        great delight
When I was writing so much myself
I wasn't afraid that what they wrote would bother me
And might even give me ideas.

I walked through the spring fountain of spring
Air fountain knowing finally that poetry was everything:
Sleep, silence, darkness, cool white air, and language

3. The Secret

Flaming
They seem
To come, sometimes,
Flaming
Despite all the old
Familiar effects
And despite my knowing
That, well, really they're not flaming
And these flaming words
Are sometimes the best ones I write
And sometimes not.

The doctor told X don't write poetry
It will kill you, which is a very late example
Of the idea of the immortal killing the man
(Not since Hector or one of those people practically)
X either wrote or didn't I don't remember—
I was writing (what made me think of it)
And my heart beat so fast
I actually thought I would die.

Our idea is something we talked about, our idea
Our idea is to write poetry that is better than poetry
To be as good as or better than the best old poetry

To evade, avoid all the mistakes of bad modern poets
Our idea is to do something with language
That has never been done before
Obviously—otherwise it wouldn't be creation
We stick to it and now I am a little nostalgic
For our idea, we never speak of it any more, it's been
Absorbed into our work, and even our friendship
Is an old, rather fragile-looking thing.
Maybe poetry took the life out of both of them,
Idea and friendship.

I like the new stuff you're doing
She wrote and then she quoted some lines
And made some funny references to the poems
And he said have you forgotten how to write the other
        kind of poems
Or, rather, she said it I forget which
I was as inspired as I have ever been
Writing half-conscious and half-unconscious every day
After taking a walk or looking at the garden
Or making love to you (as we used to say)

Unconscious meant "grace"
It meant No matter who I am
I am greater than I am
And this is greater
And this, since I am merely the vessel of it,
May be the truth

Then I read Ariosto
I fell to my knees

And started looking for the pins
I had dropped when I decided to be unconscious

I wanted to fasten everything together
As he did and make an enormous poetry Rose
Which included everything
And which couldn't be composed by the "unconscious"
(At least not by the "unconscious" alone)

This rose became a bandanna, which became a house
Which became infused with all passion, which became a
      hideaway
Which became yes I would like to have dinner, which
      became hands
Which became lands, shores, beaches, natives on the
      stones
Staring and wild beasts in the trees, chasing the hats of
Lost hunters, and all this deserves a tone
That I try to give it by writing as fast as I can
And as steadily, pausing only to eat, sleep, and as we
      used to say, make love
And take long walks, where I would sometimes en-
      counter a sheep
Which gave me rhyming material and often a flowering
      fruit tree,
Pear apple cherry blossom thing and see long paths
      winding
Up hills and then down to somewhere invisible again
Which I would imagine was a town, in which another
      scene of the poem could take place.

4. Out and In

City of eternal flowers
And A said Why not make it paternal flowers
And Z said Or sempiternal There were bananas
Lying on the closet shelf by the couch
Forty feet from where your miscarriage began
And we were talking about this nonsense
Which meant so much to us, meant so much to us at the
    time.

Ponte Vecchio going over the Arno
What an image you are this morning
In the eye of almighty God!
I am the old bridge he said she said
I forget if it was a boy or a girl
A sexless thing in my life
Like sidewalks couches and lunch

Walking around nervously then going in the house
The entire problem is to sit down
And start writing. Solved! Now the problem
Is to get up. Solved! Now the problem
Is to find something equally worthwhile to do. Solved!
Thank you for coming to see me. But
Thank you for living with me. And
Thank you for marrying me. While
Thank you for the arguments and the fights
And the deadly interpellations about the meanings of
    things!

Your blue eyes are filled with storms
To alter and mildly disarrange an image of someone's, he
    said it about the eyelid
But you are crying. I have a pain in my side.

The idea of Mallarmé
That
Well that it was so
Vital
Poetry, whatever it was
Is inspiring
Is I find even more inspiring
Than his more famous idea
Of absence
And his famous idea
Of an uncertain relationship of the words
In a line to make it memorably *fugace*.

Absence and I were often in my room
Composing. When I came out you and absence were
    wielding a broom
Which was a task I hadn't thought of in my absence
Finally absence took over
You, me, the broom, my writing, my typewriter,
Florence, the house, Katherine, everything.

Well, I don't know—those were great moments
Sometimes and terrible moments sometimes
And sometimes we went to the opera
And sometime later the automobile squeaked
There is no such thing as an automobile, there is only a
    Mercedes or a Ferrari

Or a Renault Deux Chevaux is that a Citroën
There is What do we care what kind of car but
Often in the sunshine we did. That's
When we were traveling I wasn't writing.

You've got to sit down and write. Solved!
But what I write isn't any good. Unsolved!
Try harder. Solved! No results. Unsolved!
Try taking a walk. Solved! An intelligent, pliable,
Luminous, spurting, quiet, delicate, amiable, slender line
Like someone who really loves me
For one second. What a life! (Solved!) Temporarily.

What do you think I should do
With all these old poems
That I am never going to even look at again
Or think about or revise—Throw them out!
But if I raise my hand to do this I feel like Abraham!
And no sheep's around there to prevent me.
So I take another look.

We asked the bad poet to come and dine
The bad poet said he didn't have time
The good poet came and acted stupid
He went to sleep on the couch
But grandiose inspiration had arrived for him with the
    wine
Such was the occasion.

Long afternoons, when I'm not too nervous
Or driven, I sit
And talk to the source of my happiness a little bit

Then Baby gets dressed but not in very much it's
Warm out and off we go
For twenty minutes or so and then come back.

Everyone in the neighboring houses
And in the neighboring orchards and fields
Is busily engaged in doing something
(So I imagine) as I sit here and write.

5. Days and Nights

A B C D F I J
L M N R Y and Z were the friends I had who wrote
    poetry
Now A B and C are dead, L N and Y have stopped
    writing
Z has gotten better than ever and I am in a heavy mood
Wondering how much life and how much writing there
    should be—
For me, have the two become mostly the same?
Mostly! Thank God for the mostly! Last night with you
I felt by that shaken and uplifted
In a way that no writing could ever do.
The body after all is a mountain and words are a mist—
I love the mist. Heaven help me, I also love you.

When the life leaves the body life will still be in the
    words
But that will be a little and funny kind of life
Not including you on my lap
And looking at me then shading your beautiful eyes.

Do you want me to keep telling
You things about your
Poem or do you want me to stop? Oh
Tell me. What? I don't think
You should have that phrase "burn up" in the first line.
Why not? I don't know. It
Seems a little unlike the rest.

O wonderful silence of animals
It's among you that I best perhaps could write!
Yet one needs readers. Also other people to talk to
To be friends with and to love. To go about with. And
This takes time. And people make noise,
Talking, and playing the piano, and always running
        around.

Night falls on my desk. It's an unusual situation.
Usually I have stopped work by now. But this time I'm
        in the midst of a thrilling evasion,
Something I promised I wouldn't do—sneaking in a
        short poem
In the midst of my long one. Meanwhile you're patient,
        and the veal's cold.

Fresh spring evening breezes over the plates
We finish eating from and then go out.
Personal life is everything personal life is nothing
Sometimes—click—one just feels isolated from personal
        life
Of course it's not public life I'm comparing it to, that's
        nonsense vanity—
So what's personal life? the old mom-dad-replay joke or

Sex electricity's unlasting phenomenon? That's right.
    And on
This spring evening it seems sensational. Long may it be
    lasting!

It helps me to be writing it helps me to breathe
It helps me to say anything it gives me
I'm afraid more than I give it

I certainly have lost something
My writing makes me aware of it
It isn't life and it isn't youth
I'm still young enough and alive
It's what I wrote in my poems
That I've lost, the way Katherine would walk
As far as the tree line, and how the fruit tree blossoms
Would seem to poke their way into the window
Although they were a long way outside

Yes sex is a great thing I admire it
Sex is like poetry it makes you aware of hands feet arms
    and legs
And your beating heart
I have never been inspired by sex, always by love
And so we talk about "sex" while thinking a little about
    poetry

There are very few poems
Compared to all the thought
And the activity and the sleeping and the falling in love
And out of love and the friendships
And all the talk and the doubts and the excitement

And the reputations and the philosophies
And the opinions about everything and the sensitivity
And the being alone a lot and having to be with others
A lot and the going to bed a lot and getting up a lot and
    seeing
Things all the time in relation to poetry
And so on and thinking about oneself
In this somewhat peculiar way

Well, producing a lot, that's not what
Being a poet is about, said N.
But trying to do so is certainly one of the somethings
It is about, though the products I must say are most
    numinous—
Wisps of smoke! while novels and paintings clouds go
    belching over the way!

Poetry, however, lives forever.
Words—how strange. It must be that in language
There is less competition
Than there is in regular life, where there are always
Beautiful persons being born and growing to adulthood
And ready to love. If great poems were as easy to create
    as people—
I mean if the capacity to do so were as widespread—
Since there's nothing easy about going through a
    pregnancy—
I suppose we could just forget about immortality. Maybe
    we can!

Z said It isn't poetry
And R said It's the greatest thing I ever read

And Y said I'm sick. I want to get up
Out of bed. Then we can talk about poetry
And L said There is some wine
With lunch, if you want some
And N (the bad poet) said
Listen to this. And J said I'm tired and
M said Why don't you go to sleep. We laughed
And the afternoon-evening ended
At the house in bella Firenze.

One Train May Hide Another

(*sign at a railroad crossing in Kenya*)

In a poem, one line may hide another line,
As at a crossing, one train may hide another train.
That is, if you are waiting to cross
The tracks, wait to do it for one moment at
Least after the first train is gone. And so when you read
Wait until you have read the next line—
Then it is safe to go on reading.
In a family one sister may conceal another,
So, when you are courting, it's best to have them all in
        view
Otherwise in coming to find one you may love another.
One father or one brother may hide the man,
If you are a woman, whom you have been waiting to
        love.
So always standing in front of something the other
As words stand in front of objects, feelings, and ideas.

One wish may hide another. And one person's reputation
   may hide
The reputation of another. One dog may conceal another
On a lawn, so if you escape the first one you're not
   necessarily safe;
One lilac may hide another and then a lot of lilacs and
   on the Appia Antica one tomb
May hide a number of other tombs. In love, one re-
   proach may hide another,
One small complaint may hide a great one.
One injustice may hide another—one colonial may hide
   another,
One blaring red uniform another, and another, a whole
   column. One bath may hide another bath
As when, after bathing, one walks out into the rain.
One idea may hide another: Life is simple
Hide Life is incredibly complex, as in the prose of
   Gertrude Stein
One sentence hides another and is another as well. And
   in the laboratory
One invention may hide another invention,
One evening may hide another, one shadow, a nest of
   shadows.
One dark red, or one blue, or one purple—this is a
   painting
By someone after Matisse. One waits at the tracks until
   they pass,
These hidden doubles or, sometimes, likenesses. One
   identical twin
May hide the other. And there may be even more in
   there! The obstetrician

Gazes at the Valley of the Var. We used to live there, my
    wife and I, but
One life hid another life. And now she is gone and I am
    here.
A vivacious mother hides a gawky daughter. The
    daughter hides
Her own vivacious daughter in turn. They are in
A railway station and the daughter is holding a bag
Bigger than her mother's bag and successfully hides it.
In offering to pick up the daughter's bag one finds one-
    self confronted by the mother's
And has to carry that one, too. So one hitchhiker
May deliberately hide another and one cup of coffee
Another, too, until one is over-excited. One love may
    hide another love or the same love
As when "I love you" suddenly rings false and one
    discovers
The better love lingering behind, as when "I'm full of
    doubts"
Hides "I'm certain about something and it is that"
And one dream may hide another as is well known,
    always, too. In the Garden of Eden
Adam and Eve may hide the real Adam and Eve.
Jerusalem may hide another Jerusalem.
When you come to something, stop to let it pass
So you can see what else is there. At home, no matter
    where,
Internal tracks pose dangers, too: one memory
Certainly hides another, that being what memory is all
    about,
The eternal reverse succession of contemplated entities.
    Reading *A Sentimental Journey* look around

When you have finished, for *Tristram Shandy*, to see
If it is standing there, it should be, stronger
And more profound and theretofore hidden as Santa
　　　Maria Maggiore
May be hidden by similar churches inside Rome. One
　　　sidewalk
May hide another, as when you're asleep there, and
One song hide another song; a pounding upstairs
Hide the beating of drums. One friend may hide
　　　another, you sit at the foot of a tree
With one and when you get up to leave there is another
Whom you'd have preferred to talk to all along. One
　　　teacher,
One doctor, one ecstasy, one illness, one woman, one
　　　man
May hide another. Pause to let the first one pass.
You think, Now it is safe to cross and you are hit by the
　　　next one. It can be important
To have waited at least a moment to see what was
　　　already there.

A Time Zone

On y loue des chambres en latin Cubicula locanda
Je m'en souviens j'y ai passé trois jours et autant à Gouda
APOLLINAIRE, *Zone*

A light from the ceiling is swinging outside on Forty-
　　　second Street traffic is zinging
Collaborating on The Construction of Boston is
　　　interesting

To construct the city of Boston Tinguely is putting up a
big wall
Of gray sandstone bricks he is dressed in a French ball
Gown he puts the wall up during the performance
His costume is due to art and not to mental disturbance
Now the wall ten feet high is starting to tremble
People seated in the first rows run back for shelter
However the bricks stand firm Niki de St. Phalle dressed
as Napoleon
Shoots at a Venus full of paint with a miniature (but real)
cannon
Rauschenberg's rain machine's stuck it gives too much
moisture
People look very happy to have gotten out of the theater
People ask that it be put on again but it can't be done
Tinguely with his hand bleeding says Boston can be con-
structed only once
And that is the end of that
Next day the Maidman Theatre stage is flat
I like the random absurdity of this performance
Done only once with nineteen-sixty-two-and-art
romance
I meet Niki four years earlier in France in the spring
Five years before that I am with Janice and Katherine
In Greece two thousand years ago everything came
crashing
We stand and try to imagine it from what is still standing
Years before this in Paris it's the boulevard Montparnasse
Larry Rivers is here he is living with a family that in-
cludes a dwarf
We are talking I have a "Fulbright" with us is Nell
Blaine

I am pulled in one direction by Sweden in another by
    Spain
The idea of staying in Europe jolts me gives a con-
    vincing jerk
It's New York though where most of my friends are and
    the "new work"
Today with Frank O'Hara a lunch connection
The Museum of Modern Art is showing its Arp collection
Frank comes out of the doorway in his necktie and his
    coat
It is a day on which it would be good to vote
Autumn a crisp Republicanism is in the air tie and coat
Soon to be trounced by the Democrats personified as a
    slung-over-the-shoulder coat
Fascism in the form of a bank
Gives way to a shining restaurant that opens its doors
    with a clank
However before being taken into this odoriferous coffer
A little hard-as-a-hat poem to the day we offer
"Sky/woof woof !/harp"
This is repeated ten times
Each word is one line so the whole poem is thirty lines
It's a poem composed in a moment
On the sidewalk about fifteen blocks from the Alice in
    Wonderland Monument
Sky woof woof! harp is published in *Semicolon*
Later than this in this John Myers publication
O'Hara meanwhile is bending above his shirt
His mind being and putting mine on being on Inter-
    national Alert
There's no self-praise in his gossip

Which in fact isn't gossip but like an artistic air-trip
To all the greatest monuments of America and Europe
Relayed in a mild excited wide open-eyed smiling con-
versational style
Larry he says and Larry again after a while
He is crazy about Larry these two have a relationship
That is breaking the world's record for loquaciousness
 I first meet Larry on Third Avenue
The El goes past and it throws into my apartment rust
dust soot and what-have-you
Larry has a way of putting himself all out in front of
himself
And stumbling through it and looking good while
seemingly making fun of himself
This is my friend Larry Rivers says Jane Freilicher
She lives upstairs Larry is a sometime visitor
He is dedicated at this moment entirely to drawing
Abstract split-splot and flops and spots he finds a blur
and boring
Give me a glass of pencil that hath been
Steeped a long time in Delacroix and Ingres nor does he
neglect Rubens
He is drawing up a storm in his studio working hard
A little bit earlier he and Jane and others are bouleversés
by Bonnard
Bonnard show at the Modern Museum
I meet these people too late to go and see them
I am of New York not a native
I'm from Cincinnati which is to this place's nominative
like a remote dative
In 1948 from college I come here and finally settle

The city is hot and bright and noisy like a giant boiling
kettle
My first connection to it aside from touristy is sexual
A girl met here or there at first nothing serious or
contextual
That is earlier now I'm here to live on street subway and
bus
I find people exciting unrecognizable and of unknown-
to-me social class
Finally they start to come into focus
For a while it's like being at a play I may have the wrong
tickets
On West Tenth Street now I am firmly settled in New
York
I am a poet je suis poète but I'm not doing very much
work
I'm in love with a beautiful girl named Robin
Her father has a hand-weaving factory he gives me a job
winding bobbins
It is a one-floor loft in the garment district on Thirty-
first Street
Pat Hoey visits someone next door on snow-white feet
Pat and I like to go to the ballet at the City Center
I get "Balanchined" as in a wine-press all Jacques
d'Amboise has to do is enter
My poetry is somewhat stuck
It's taking me a little while to be able to write in New York
My painter friends help and what I am reading in the
library
It is not the contemporary antics this happens later of
John Ashbery

This shy and skinny poet comes down to visit me from
"school"
When he and Jane Freilicher meet it's as if they'd both
been thrown into a swimming pool
Afloat with ironies jokes sensitivities perceptions and
sweet swift sophistications
Like the orchids of Xochimilco a tourist attraction for
the nations
Jane is filled with excitement and one hundred percent
ironic
This conversation is joy is speed is infinite gin and tonic
It is modernism in the lyrical laconic
Our relationship's platonic
With what intelligence linked to what beauty linked to
what grassy gusty lurch across the canvas
Jane and her paintings I realize once again happiness
Huh? is possibly going to be available after long absence
Here today in a gray raincoat she appears
The style is laughter the subject may be a cause for tears
Larry has some of the qualities of a stand-up comic
He says of John Myers John Myers he always calls him
that
John Myers never John John Myers says he isn't fat
Well doesn't have a fat EAR but look at his stomach
And oft at a party back his head he throws
And plays the piano singing a song he made up "My
Nose"
His nose bothers and is thus conquered by Larry Rivers
He's doing a Bonnardesque painting it's so good it gives
me "recognition" shivers
It's a room filled with women with somewhat beautiful
fishlike graces

Mostly orangey-yellow they have sexy and sleepy looks
     on their faces the thick
Oil paint makes it look as if you'd stick
To it if you got next to it it also looks very spacious
Now Larry is sitting and smiling he is copying an Ingres
His hand is shaky his lines are as straight as coat hangers
Why don't you I say rather dumbly put something witty
     in your work
No Kenneth I can't he says prancing around like a funny
     Turk
Charcoal in one hand and making a little gesture with
     the other
One Sunday I go with him to the Bronx to visit his sister
     and his mother
Here I am with Larry's sister and his mother
Sitting in the kitchen above us is a motto
Joannie is blonde her brunette friend is warm and
     flushed as a risotto
I rather fancy her and Larry's mother fancies it stupid
To have invited this girl at the same time as me so inter-
     rupting the arrow of Cupid
Posing for Rivers his mother-in-law Berdie before a
     screen
Posing for her son-in-law this woman full and generous
     as the double issue of a magazine
The French *Vogue* for example or the *Ladies' Home Journal*
Frank thinks her marvelous he finds the sublime in her
     diurnal
Larry is making a leafy tree out of metal
Here is his Jewish version of Courbet's painting of a
     funeral
Jane loves Matisse and is a fan of Baudelaire

In these paintings she is working on a secret of yellow
	blue and pink air
She and Larry make a big painting together
Larry with an unmeditated slash Jane with the per-
	petuity of a feather
That in a breeze is trying to pull itself together
I'm looking at the finished product it's rather de
	Kooningesque
Being de-Kooning-like some way is practically of being
	a New York painter the test
Here today though is not a de Kooning but one of Jane's
	it's luscious big and feminine
I am inspired by these painters
They make me want to paint myself on an amateur basis
Without losing my poetic status
Jane is demonstrating to me the pleasures of using
	charcoal
I am copying a Delacroix of a black woman called I
	think The Slave Girl
Erasing makes a lovely mess
It looks like depth and looks like distance
Ink at the opposite end of materials is deliberate and
	daring
No chance to erase it and oil pastels like wildflowers in a
	clearing
My Aesthetic I only paint for a few years is rather
	elementary
Get something that looks good looks real looks sur-
	prising looks from this century
I am sitting at a little table downstairs in the Third
	Avenue apartment
I like buying slabs of masonite and all kinds of equipment

At the Metropolitan on a big wall is a great big Rubens
Of a king and some nobles on horses bigger than cabins
I am walking through the European Collection
With Larry and Jane they're giving it a professional
    inspection
On drawing paper I'm doing some Seurat-like dotting
I like this even love it but I know it's going to come to
    nothing
It is invigorating to stand in this studio
John Ashbery comes to visit he is listening to Bob and
    Ray on our radio
It is a small old-fashioned console attacked by salt water
John finds them wheezingly amusing all over the house
    sounds his raucous laughter
He and I "go back" to Harvard College
Now he is sitting at his typewriter in Greenwich Village
He's just finished a poem and he's happy as after a good
    repast
He is certain this feeling won't last
John is predictably and pleasantly gloom-filled
I've just driven to New York from some place north of
    Bloomfield
I'm an hour and a half late
This enables John to finish his poem as I with mixed
    feelings find out
"The Picture of Little J. A. in a Prospect of Flowers"
He made good use of this couple of wasted hours
Dick gives Genevieve a swift punch in the pajamas
It's a vault over W. C. Williams and a bypass of Dylan
    Thomas
He is still sitting at his little portable

Being because of my poem-causing lateness exception-
ally cordial
We are both fans of the old Mystery Plays
We also find each other mysterious in certain ways
This mystery becomes greater as more time passes
Then finally the mystery itself passes
We're at Harvard together
We walk along talking about poetry in the autumn
weather
He is not writing much this year but he likes to
collaborate
So do I we do a set of sestinas at a speedy rate
Six sestinas each about an animal with one concluding
one called The Bestiary
There is also a three-page poem in which all the lines
rhyme with the title The Cassowary
Next we do a poetic compendium called The New York
Times
September Eighth Nineteen Fifty-One both with and
without rhymes
Our poems are like tracks setting out
We have little idea where we're going or what it's about
I enjoy these compositional duets
Accompanied by drinking coffee and joking on Charles
and Perry Streets
We tell each other names of writers in great secret
Secret but absolutely no one else cares so why keep it
We're writing a deliberately bad work called The
Reconstruction of Colonial Williamsburg
In a feeble attempt to win a contest the style is the
Kenyon Review absurd

Larry and Jane propose to me renting a house in East
  Hampton
We go sizzling out of the city with the rapidity of a flu
  symptom
No this is actually a year later my memory missed it
I now go to California to be a "teaching assistant"
This year goes by I meet the girl who is later my wife
  Janice
I love to kiss her and to talk to her very often it's talking
  about my friends
I also talk a lot about "Europe" and France
She's a little deflating and tells me that to be a great poet
I have to do something she tells me but I forget exactly
  what
I think have for all my poems some sort of system
I am shaken but still feel secure in my avant-garde wisdom
East Hampton glaringest of Hamptons Hampton of sea
  shine of de Kooning and of leaves
Frank's visiting we're composing a poem he tugs at his
  sleeves
It is a Nina we are composing it is a Nina Sestina
For Nina Castelli's birthday her adorable sixteenth one
This year this month this week in fact Frank writes
  "Hatred"
A stunning tour-de-poem on an unending roll of paper
It makes going on forever seem attractive
Writing in the manner of O'Hara means being
  extremely active
Twenty people are over then thirty now about forty
Zip Frank sits down in the midst and types out a poem it
  doesn't even seem arty

I try it out with little success
It's one of those things the originator can do best
"Hatred" is full of a thundering array of vocables
From it straight through to the Odes Frank's talent is
	implacable
Now here he is holding out to me a package
Of Picayunes he taps one on his kneebone-covering
	khakis
Finally we have a poem for Castelli's daughter
Moonlight dissolve next day we're visiting Anne and
	Fairfield Porter
Fairfield is in his studio a mighty man
Posing like fluttering then settling sea birds around him
	Jerry Katie Elizabeth and Anne
He has opinions that do not waver
On his canvases he creates a bright and wholesome fever
Flowers like little pockets of yellow and pink pigment
Are aspiring up to a tree or a wall or a house like a
	sunlight shipment
At a John Cage concert there is hardly a sound
It's the paradise of music lost and music found
I find it pure and great as if a great big flash of light were
	going off underground
Satie and Webern are hitting me in the head and so
	finally with the Cantos is Ezra Pound
Frank and I are writing very long poems
Long is really the operative word for these poems
His is called Second Avenue mine When the Sun Tries
	to Go On
I don't know where I got the title
I'm working on it every afternoon the words seem to me
	arriving like stampeding cattle

It's not at all clear but for the first time in my life the
    words seem completely accurate
If I write for three hours I allow myself a cigarette
I'm smoking it's a little too much I'm not sure I can get
    through it alone
Frank and I read each other segments of these long
    works daily on the phone
Janice finds it funny now that I've dropped this bunch of
    pages
That I can't get them back in the right order well I do
    but it's by stages
It is April I have a job at the Hunter College Library
I come down to the Cedar on a bus hoping to see
    O'Hara and Ashbery
Astonishingly on the bus I don't know why it's the only
    occasion
I write a poem Where Am I Kenneth? It's on some
    torn-out notebook pages
The Cedar and the Five Spot each is a usable place
A celebrated comment Interviewer What do you think
    of space? De Kooning Fuck space!
In any case Frank is there he says he likes Where Am I
    Kenneth?
I carry this news home pleasantly and the poem it
    mentions her to Janice
John's poem Europe is full of avant-garde ardor
I am thinking it's making an order out of a great disorder
I wonder at what stage in life does this get harder
The Cedar Bar one hardly thinks of it is what may be
    called a scene
However one closed to the public since no one goes
    there to be seen

It is a meeting place for the briefest romances
And here is Norman Bluhm at the bar saying Who cares
about those nances?
And here he is shoving and here is de Kooning and there
is a beer
Being flung at someone Arnold Weinstein or me
through the smoke-talky atmosphere
Of this corner booth
Voici Guston and Mitchell and Smith and here on top of
everything is Ruth
Kligman being bedazzling without stop
She writes a poem with the line At the bar you've got to
be on top
Meanwhile tonight Boris Pasternak
Is awarded the Nobel Prize and is forced to give it back
Frank O'Hara is angry there seems both a flash and a
blur in his eyes
Kenneth we've got to do something about Pasternak and
the Nobel Prize
What? well we ought to let him know
That we support him Off flies a cable into the perpetual
snow
Dear Boris Pasternak We completely support you and
we also love your early work
Signed puzzlingly for him in the morning's glare if he
ever receives it Frank O'Hara and Kenneth Koch
Staging George Washington Crossing the Delaware
Alex Katz comes up looking like a pear
He has some white plywood boards with him he says
where
Shall I put this stuff and a big bare

Wall is the side of their emplacement No chair
For Alex painting and cutting And now they're there
The seven soldiers one cherry tree one Delaware
    crossing boat
Hey hey Ken cries Alex I've done it
I've made you a set for George Washington Crossing
    the Delaware
The British and American armies face each other on
    wooden feet
I write this play in our apartment on Commerce Street
I am working in the early afternoon and stay up late
Dawn is peeling oranges on top of the skyscrapers
On the stage a wall goes up and then it's taken down
And under the Mirabeau Bridge flows the Seine
Today Larry and Frank are putting together "Stones"
It's a series of lithographs
Larry puts down blotches violently they look like the
    grapes of wrath
Frank is smoking and looking his best ideas come in
    transit
I walk the nine blocks to the studio he says Come in
New York today is white dirty and loud like a snow-
    clogged engine
Huge men in undershirts scream at each other in trucks
    near Second Avenue and Tenth Street
De Kooning's landscapey woman is full of double-
    exposure perfections
Bob Goodnough is making some small flat red corrections
Jane is concentrating she's frowning she has a look of
    happy distress

She's painting her own portrait in a long-sleeved dark
     pink dress
I'm excited I'm writing at my typewriter it doesn't make
     too much sense

Straits

To Viktor Shklovsky (and containing some of his sentences)

It is easy to be cruel in love: one merely has not to love.
Mayakowsky entered the Revolution as he would his
     own home. He went right in and began opening
     windows. How serious is it
That something final be accomplished before it is too
     late?
One entered the earth. One started flinging up
     diamonds.
They are valuable because they are few not because they
     are old.
Sitting with Harry in Venice in Loredana's living room
It was easy to be amusing about France. One merely had
     not to be present
There but in Venice instead. And all that the other
     guests said to me
How inaccurate or accurate or part of some meaningful
     or unmeaningful or cruel or stupid or worthwhile
     or happy and life-and-love-giving life they seem
     and related to literature
"A house is at the opera" "Likely it won't be on time,"
     "Town's bridges" "I love,"

Wrote Mayakowsky. It was time to disappear into a
    group of three
And not either be one or a twosome for all eternity.
In this way one could avoid love. Civilization has
    reached a certain point.
When it had reached a lesser point was the time of one's
    father
Who seemed a greater point by filling the horizon.
    Water slopped on the walks.
The women wear high-heeled shoes and talk about
    Christ. "They say he is sure to come back."
    "When?" "I don't know!"
It has never been any man's total destiny to be a father.
    To this, God may be the only exception.
But when God was a man he was a Son.
Many race to be first. Giselle doesn't move. The road
    passes through oak trees. Some trees are pink when
    in bloom.
New strategies for naval warfare have been worked out
That show that most maneuvers are irrelevant. The
    most important thing is the first engagement.
Gide entered the stables as he would his own home. He
    went right in and began opening gates. It was like a
    billiards room—with six tables.
A bird may fly through a window directly into a cage.
Bankers are people without a homeland. They live in
    apartments that look like oriental bath houses.
They collect china and occasionally say something witty.
    We are pleased when they come to visit us. The
    days pass away like a shower.
They are accompanied by actresses, who say, "The
    world is a gentle place."

I will never marry. Oh but you must marry. It's the only
    way to bear a legitimate son.
An illegitimate son is fine with me. I don't want to
    marry. It is easy to lie down on the stones.
The knife craves a throat. The hangman's noose is
    giddier than a razor.
She goes away. When he comes back to meet her the
    curtains are yellow.
They are folded, in pleats. You say to me "It is all over."
    It is all over at home.
As soon as you say "It is not all over" it is no longer all
    over at home.
We had to hoist a sail into a new wind. The movie star
    and the novelist
Are dead still not knowing anything, the scientist who
    improved our lives
And the German shepherd also who brought us delight
    for years.
Windows are broken and some have been boarded over.
    It is easy to be a glazier to the young
Harder to be a plasterer to the old. Not only the strong
    but the weak leave a legacy. They show life is not
    gone
When half gone. The man with the broken leg in the
    swimming pool is an encouraging sight. It is Andy.
Andy is it really safe for you to be swimming alone to-
    day? Yes, he replies. I am looking for a strait,
A way from this pool into the sea. If he cannot have
    everything, he will have something.
The birds also found it possible to make an adjustment.
    They took fresh views of the clouds.

One flew over here, one flew under there. An orchestra
    conductor raised his glove

To throw it to a woman in the first row. The city was
    sunny because no smoke rose from the chimneys.

Unchallenged, everyone remained alive. Once the boat
    started moving, some did not.

He saw the old way of life as a bunker that had to be
    stormed.

Do you remember the idea "Revolution"? planning for
    and waiting for the revolution?

A painter took over Venice's outdoor cafés as his own
    private particular province.

This was true for three and a half months even though
    his paintings were not very good

By objective standards. For a while he had a certain
    panache.

The world lives through long periods of drudgery so it
    can enjoy one splendid space.

The great, dutiful buildings had no tendency to fall
    down. But one bomb or one rocket

Could change their sunny adolescence. What building
    cares if it is knocked down?

The facade longs for a bombshell, the infrastructure for
    an air raid.

It was daylight in the apartment. I usually visited there
    in the evening.

Magellan sailed along the shore of America, looking for
    straits.

He sailed into the wide estuaries of rivers, but there he
    found that it was fresh water.

Fresh water meant no straits. Straits would be filled with
    salt water. But there were bays.

Magellan solved his problem of circling America but he
　　didn't return home alive. He went in and began
　　testing estuaries.

At noon he was on a coastline looking for a channel to
　　another ocean. Vales of rocks. But there are bays.
　　They are panoramas.

Magellan had to hoist a new sail. Once it was hoisted he
　　had to find a briny path.

The wind roars like a madman. Magellan goes to sleep.
　　When he wakes up it is the Pacific.

Birds stand on the deck. They are Indians.

One does not die of love unrequited but of ceasing to
　　love. Chaliapin sings. The audience sits down.

The Zairians sold the machinery from the Belgian
　　coppermines. No more copper could be pulled
　　from the earth.

Belgians had to be called back. Their cruelty was
　　equaled only by their mining expertise. They were
　　nasty colonialists but good miners.

The sun shines on the rolling water and also on the
　　marble tiles. The penguins were replaced by Indians.

We are looking for a shortcut.

The tree doesn't exist in a metaphysical world. The
　　roots crave water, the trunk is ready for an axe.

At that time I was a Futurist.

Mark Twain loved his double, Huck Finn. He loved him
　　more than himself.

He never did renounce him. When Hyperion wakes up
　　the world is already full of sun.

Nonetheless it doesn't seem true what a Swiss banker
　　said to me in Haute Savoie one evening: "Banking
　　is just like poetry."

There were painted red tiles. Here and there were inter-
spersed some blue ones. A few were green or white.
The sky was old by then: the morning and evening
papers were interchangeable.
One gives money for a work by Velasquez—not to pay
Velasquez for the time he spent painting the work
But to pay the countless others who couldn't do it—to
cover their costs.
We have to find straits but instead we find intelligence.
Why did you hurt your leg? Freud asks his son.
The moon rises over the inland ocean even on revolu-
tionary holidays.
In love, as in art, we pay for failures. We thank one indi-
vidual for the success of humanity.
Freud's son didn't know what to say to his father. Other
people's troubles are easy to bear.
Neither the bankers nor the women they went out with
were interested in marriage. They thought it the
ruin of love.
Mayakowsky was sure of himself as long as he was in
action.
Unable to break out of his style of painting, Velasquez
painted five hundred canvases.
Eventually his stylistic problem was solved—by another
painter.
The actor started speaking words as if they were his own
And not those of Shakespeare or of de Montherlant or
of Chaliapin.
Looking up at the hilly shore, he saw the fires made by
Indians.
He supposed a name for the peninsula: Tierra del Fuego.

But what if it were not a peninsula? The birds might
then be presumed to go further away.
They were used to seeing it only in the afternoon.
"With these you can start a new life." She gave him her
jewels.
Conversation is one thing in the South and another in
the North.
In the North one keeps moving.
In China, they risked banishment or prison if they
talked. This then was changed but not completely
changed.
The opening up of freedom takes place in steps:
First one speaks of the ocean, then of the boats, then of
the people on the boats, lastly of their ideas.
The fishstore man praises the young woman's smile and
her clothing. What munitions makers do is to
diversify. There are annuals.
Magellan sent an Indian boy to pick some before they
had faded; when he came back,
Magellan had decided. "We'll call it Tierra del Fuego."
The sun rose high over the fourth or fifth inland ocean
he had seen. At home in Europe he had been a shy
student,
Thought lazy and not very good with girls. When he set
off, however,
Flags from every nation and of every color adorned the
flagpoles
And the tallest masts of the highest ships of the world.
And Magellan went
As Mayakowsky went, and as Mark Twain and Cicero
went, into the future. He stood on a promontory.

Bankers predicted flax was on the rise and, with it, maize
and broccoli.

It's not true that all predictions are false. But it is true
that those who make them don't know if they are
or not.

Pushkin and Lermontov and Gogol waited on the book-
shelf for Mayakowsky—

If people were on the moon, they could have seen, for
one second, a new world.

Then just as suddenly Mayakowsky re-became a book;
his covers were like penguins.

The hot vibrations of his poetry flamed and calmed
down. They wandered around the apartments

Looking for girls who spoke their own language. Some
were fond of saying,

You don't really need to know more than a few words,
maybe not even that.

Ponce de Leon noticing his graying beard in the mirror

Said, "I know what I have to find!" He set off, but he
never found the Fountain of Youth.

Poniatowsky once found something he thought re-
sembled it: a railroad station.

He was fascinated by the choice of different directions.
But he aged anyway. By then Ponce de Leon was
gone.

He imagines a woman who is like a strait, into a cold
happiness, which is like a sea.

Cranes looking down see only fragments, gay Twombly-
like interrupted scrambles.

Thenceforth we didn't write our work in regular lines

But in staffs, like music. Satie came out and sat at the
mendicant's door.

Gandhi said, "I didn't know I had a door! Now I need no
    longer be wandering!"
They were waiting for a foot; and, after the foot, a leg;
    and then a staff.
Life brims with music when a country is founded
Or merges with another, or is diversified, like the
    Dionne Quintuplets. Cicero gave his best speeches
When he was a drunk, and Horace wrote his finest poems.
    There were no brothels: property tax had gone up.
Zeus was not a god but a projection of human con-
    sciousness. We live in the consequences
Of what we imagine persons like Gandhi have done.
The portholes looked like windows of a shop in which
    they were selling the ocean—
How much do you want for this? how much for that?
Eskimos are amazed at the size of the apartments. They
    think that they must be places to keep the dogs.
They are uninterested in politics but fascinated by the
    apartments.
No casino was opened because no one was rich—
One night's losses could ruin a person for the rest of his
    or her life.
For Poniatowsky, gambling was displaced to love—also
    for everyone he knew.
Bankers invested heavily in Magellan's voyage and their
    money was never paid back.
They invested in something that might pay off centuries
    in the future.
Magellan returned dead although he had circled South
    America.
One banker's girlfriend walked in freezing weather all
    the way from another district

To see Mayakowsky. But he was never at home. She
installed herself in his apartment.

Her banker came there looking for her; she met him at
the door.

She said, "There is no going backward in a revolution. A
revolution is like a devaluation of currency.

It is what it is and it happens when it happens." He said
"You will never win the love of Mayakowsky."

She said that that however was what she wanted.

The idea of installing a phone booth to some seemed
central.

People wished to communicate. The sight of a phone
booth was like a whiff of salt air, from the sea.

The plan of having a Doge as governor was quickly
abandoned—it was impractical

From every point of view. The china belonged to an ad-
miral. Forty-five years ago he had gone to school

With Yesenin's father. He had padded shoulders, like a
football player; he was sturdy but short.

We came to see him to ask help for an artistic project; he
was amiable but unresponsive.

In a civilization one has to be Mark Twain or André
Eglevsky or, at the limit, Lord Byron.

Shakespeare looked in a mirror. It was much more
bracing to open a window:

There one could see only what one was not. Prospero
found Ferdinand as a husband for Miranda.

Once Shakespeare had written the play the subject was
dead.

I had seen the apartment only in the afternoon or early
evening.

Once I had done that, it was easier to see what had to be
    done.
Music didn't sound to Orpheus as it did to Rilke.
    Orpheus took it for granted
As a natural thing and an accompaniment to words.
    Parliament was convened.
"When were you here last?" Napoleon whispered to his
    horse.
When his horse didn't reply, Napoleon smiled, and rode
    him into battle. When his horse died, he wept.
I didn't know you were living near this pool! "Oh, I
    don't," said Andy; "to swim here I come a long way
Past shops and market stalls—I am looking for a strait."
    But there is none in this pool, Andy. Humanity is
    astonished
By the successes it contains and tends to celebrate the
    failures
Until a new explanation comes to light.
Mayakowsky imagined he saw a wolf in the long
    Moscow night
But actually he committed suicide. The deed was signed
    but no one had looked at the property.
The sun went into the west opening up portholes. These
    were stars
At which you could buy the Ascension.
Books were a scarcity. A man would fold up a newspaper
    and read it as a book. The ice lasted
Until spring. The orchestra was conducted
By a former slave but everyone was free when Chaliapin
    sang. During the Cold War
Forgetfulness was almost a necessity, it was difficult to
    live without it.

I made friends with a member of the Russian embassy. I
    asked him if he was an attaché or the ambassador.
The Russian only nodded grimly and walked into the
    canal.
The newspapers next day reported Mayakowsky's death
As an accident. The Apollos had an "archaic smile"—
    one theory was that there existed a happiness
At that time in that place that never existed anyplace else.
Wallace Stevens thought to find it in Florida, taking the
    boat
Across the Gulf to Havana, where he would find com-
    pliant young women. This was the source of many
    of his poems.
El Greco lived in Seville but wasn't a Spaniard
But a Greek. As was the case with Christ, his name
    designated what, not who, he was.
There was a phone booth about every half mile. Magel-
    lan had an address book
With nothing in it. He had burned all his past relation-
    ships. He might not have recognized Chaliapin
As a great singer. But he was going to the South Pole
Whether anyone wanted him to or not. The "archaic
    smile" is attributed by others,
Like Disney's use of four-fingered gloves, to the relative
    easiness of making things that way, a smile is easier
    to draw
Than a ruminative or prescient expression. A proletarian
    navy
Seemed a contradiction, like ordinary eyes with an
    avant-garde nose.
One had to be a "Lombardi" to work on the church. He
    wanted to detain autumn.

It was departing. It took the drapes down from the trees,
Threw everything on the floor, started packing.
Autumn was holding its gun to the head of the willows.
The streetcar tracks brought syphilis to the door. Tall
and sometimes blissful
She was running around his apartment dressed in fabric.
At the end of the month, when the rent came due, she
got on a bus
And went to the Vatican. The linden's leaves dried. A
notice came again
For the rent. Convicted intellectuals were confined to a
room and allowed only one book per month.
The captain changed into a dinner jacket. On holidays,
the villagers would choose up sides and fight.
Walt Whitman wrote, There was never any more per-
fection than there is now.
When he looked out the window he saw the sun.
Poetry burned on tables. Whitman wrote flattering
reviews of himself. A German scholar
Who up till that time had been a fervent admirer,
changed, when he found this out,
And became a ferocious detractor. He confused what
Whitman was with what Whitman wrote.
If Giselle lay down, the people danced over her. She has
on a vest of aqua.
But there are bays. Andy is carving his way through one
of them, hand over hand.
The Doge acknowledged that trade was bad. He went
back in and began opening up trade routes.
Later he was deposed, an old man who was too fond of
young women. But no one else could be found at
his level.

Venice remained ungoverned for forty years. It could
thank one of its leaders for the success of its trade
routes.

When the rat came out from behind the curtain it
seemed no longer a rat

But it was—it just happened that the sunlight had
disguised it as a ball of yarn.

It was easy to be a signer of the Constitution. One
merely had to be there.

Youth gave power to some people, and money gave
power to others.

Some spent their youth devising theories, others on
experiencing sex

With as many persons as possible. Only a small minority
were fascinated by estuaries.

Music was defined by Tchaikowsky as "disappearing
youth." When he wrote music, it stopped
disappearing.

The ocean is a source of elegies and a popular location
for casinos.

There wasn't money for people to spend on taking taxis.
The taxi drivers didn't blame them.

They felt, correctly, that they were stuck in a proletarian
society

With providing an aristocratic mode of transportation.
They took their plight with some humor.

Occasionally a banker took a cab and spent a lot of
money. He was paying not for the ride he got

But for the availability of the service. What if the revolu-
tion were like a taxi

And couldn't be afforded? We say that life is beautiful

Not only to pay a compliment to something in which we
are already included
But to separate inside and outside, if only for a moment.
Shklovsky said, "I speak in a voice grown hoarse from
silence and pamphlets."
It didn't pay him to be wrong about the Soviet State and
it didn't pay him to be right.
He said, "Spring was creeping under coats and over
bosoms," and "Quiet and fat, I ran around in a
shiny black jacket."
With style, he opposed the state. "Death is not the worst
of all sorrows," said the Italian
Who came to fix Shklovsky's clock. This clock was stuck
at quarter after eleven.
Elsa didn't call back. He spoke of the factory.
No one was supposed to comment on the failings of
Soviet industry.
Putilov has an area of fifty square miles and a population
of thirty-five thousand.
Most of these people work in the plant. The plant makes
a tremendous amount of noise but produces very
little.
The machines are out-of-date and not well taken care
of. Thus the clatter.
Mayakowsky opened windows. Shklovsky wrote,
"Noise is work for an orchestra, but not for the Putilov
plant."
He spent a number of years in exile. "It is supposed to
be turning out products."

Currency

In the Fifties Western Europe was the place
That had just been through a war. The currencies were
    wobbly.
A run-down American student could live like Wallace
    Stevens
Among the moguls of Hartford. This was helpful for
    poetry
If bad for a lot else. Not many French apartments had
    bathrooms,
Almost none refrigerators. One went to the public baths
    and looked out
The already steamed-up windows at the city.
I sat around a lot in Montparnasse
Cafés—you know them, the Select, the Dôme, and
The Rotonde. The Rotonde those days stayed open
All night. The old-fashioned French coffee machine was
    steaming.
It gave off an awful and awfully exciting smell.
The Surrealists were aging, like the paper of their books
Le paysan de Paris and *Les malheurs des immortels*
Above—up there—the river is winding. The museum is
    full of busts
Its large paintings are like days.
A friend was foreign and far away.
Everyone understands these things but no one is looking.
The fire escapes are in New York with everyone else.
Important here is to get my foot on the street
Before the car gets there. From the asphalt gas and
    steam not going up.
However, there is a book store on the rue de Rennes.

Its French books are very cheap.

A book costs hardly more than a postcard in the United
States.

This situation is temporary. Meanwhile I am becoming
well-read

In modern French poetry. I also read *La chanson de
Roland* translated into Modern French

And Virgil's *Eclogues* and his *Georgics* translated into
French.

They seem to make more sense to me than in English.

I find it in the air as well as in Max Jacob,

In Jouve and in de Montherlant. Surrealism is bouquet
to these arrogated French tables.

Who thinks about those things.

I am away from ghostly and boasting New York.

In the bookstore I meet Henri Michaux. The kind man
who owns the bookstore introduces me to him

He thinks we may both like it

I more than Henri Michaux. I like it.

I am nervous I am some kind of phantom.

No don't buy the Larousse buy this a truly serious dic-
tionary a man under the sidewalk in his papery
dusty crowded store says to me

But I am not that scholarly American

I am learning from Paris's streets to lead a life without
consequence

But isn't that a life of consequence?

It is not very often that I get around to love-making

Not in this first early year.

Sexual passion and excitement are more interesting to
me when I am older.

They interested me every year.

I am not studying this but Je t'aime and je vais jouir

I'm learning French phrases but I feel mystified and off
to the side

I notice her long thin arms she wants to be an airline
stewardess

If I held on long enough I'd be perhaps somewhat
"French"

I want to be famous amidst the prose of everyday
existence

In fact this year I don't care about fame

I have never cared about it I just want to be delighted
and I'm envious

I want to be part of that enormous cake over there

That is a monument being wheeled down les Champs
Elysées

I am daft about Paris's white sidewalks

Everything I have read and done since then

Is not more real. I wrote I completely forget what.

One friend said this version (#2) is "more abstract" than
this (1st) one. I said Thank you.

Michaux was pleasant with me, and witty.

Invisible the monstrous sufferer of his poetry

Whereas my overexcited feeling is all too evident.

I am twenty-five years old and in good health sleeping

I'm sitting in a smoky restaurant

Thanksgiving Day Sixth Arrondissement I was not
eating turkey

Or cranberry sauce but some petits suisses

These are very petits but are they suisses in what ways
are they suisses

The conversation's booming around me

I feel lost in this breaking ocean of French happiness-
    inducing culinary indulgence
These fat bourgeois I am a thin bourgeois only because I
    am twenty-five
Giacometti is sitting drinking at the Dôme. He is with
    his followers.
I have a bicycle. I try but I can't hear one word that
    Giacometti says.
How long ago is it that I started to "dream in French"?
    Two months.
I want to be something else. I keep listening.
Life isn't infinite.
Now it may seem infinite but it isn't infinite.
Minor ailments don't interfere with my struggle to
    become French.
I will never become French.
I like too much being American. Also partly French.
Jean Cocteau equals Juan Gris. They even have, almost,
    the same name.
Birds ce sont les oiseaux.
Here I am in Paris being miserably lonely. All the same.
All the same even Amadis de Gaul knew when it was
    time to go home.
When he had conquered his enemies.
I have not yet conquered France.
By the time I get close to it I think death may have
    conquered me.
My first "moment" on French soil which is the soil of
    Normandy
The ship the Degrasse lands and I put down my foot
On some sparsely grown grass mud that leads up to the
    platform where the train

Is that will be taking me to Paris
To Montparnasse its beds are its streets
Its pillows the cafés. I am streetless in the Hôtel de
    Fleurus
Then I came down from there.
My mail is at American Express.
I have a friend who will not be my friend for very long.
And many, unknown, I have yet to meet.
What will it matter? It matters that I am not alone.
It matters that someone agrees
And that there are walls like energy.
I am unaware of a lot that has gone on here—the herding
    of the Jews
Into railroad cars, to Belsen.
I read Max Jacob "La rue Ravignan" in
Le cornet à dés with its conclusion "c'est toi, Dostoievski"
In the road I pick up leaves in the street I pick up books
Max Jacob who had long ago proofread the last page of
    his *The Central Laboratory*
Is dead, killed by the Nazis.
Now Larry like a clown down the street
It's extremely late and Nell we three meet
And drink coffee
It tastes like dirt or metal, hot and steaming, like the
    whole world that's coming to be,
The coffee of our lives, the strong and bitter café de nos
    vies.
The yellow and pink lines come marching down the
    boulevard Montparnasse
We can pay for the coffee so we have the dawn.

Songs from the Plays

Your genius made me shiver
It seemed to me
That you were greater than I
Could ever be
Your genius made me shiver.

Pure genius makes us shiver
We who want to be
Torn out of history
And raised up to be
Intellectual heroes.

How easily you do
What I must work to do
Long and long hours
How quickly you renew
Your much-spent powers.

Your genius makes to shiver
All those who have forever
Longed, longed for the caress
Of glory and the Muses
Who, all, know now that they shall have it less

Than you shall have it, ever—
Illumined, and onrushing like a river.

from *Brothers and Friends*

You want a social life, with friends,
A passionate love life and as well
To work hard every day. What's true
Is of these three you may have two
And two can pay you dividends
But never may have three.

There isn't time enough, my friends—
Though dawn begins, yet midnight ends—
To find the time to have love, work, and friends.
Michelangelo had feeling
For Vittoria and the Ceiling
But did he go to parties at day's end?

Homer nightly went to banquets
Wrote all day but had no lockets
Bright with pictures of his Girl.
I know one who loves and parties
And has done so since his thirties
But writes hardly anything at all.

from *Brothers and Friends*

To "Yes"

You are always the member of a team,
Accompanied by a question—
If this is the way the world ends, is it really going to?
No. Are you a Buddhist? Maybe. A monsoon? Yes.

I have been delighted by you even in the basement
When asking if I could have some coal lumps and the
    answer was yes.
Yes to the finality of the brightness
And to the enduring qualities of the lark
She sings at heaven's gate. But is it unbolted? Bolted?
    Yes.
Which, though, is which? To which the answer cannot
    be yes
So reverse question. Pamela bending before the grate
Turns round rapidly to say Yes! I will meet you in
    Boston
At five after nine, if my Irishness is still working
And the global hamadryads, wood nymphs of my "yes."
But what, Pamela, what does that mean? Am I a yes
To be posed in the face of a negative alternative?
Or has the sky taken away from me its ultimate guess
About how probably everything is going to be eventually
    terrible
Which is something we knew all along, being modified
    by a yes
When what we want is obvious but has a brilliantly
    shining trail
Of stars. Or are those asterisks? Yes. What is at the
    bottom
Of the most overt question? Do we die? Yes. Does that
Always come later than now? Yes.
I love your development
From the answer to a simple query to a state of peace
That has the world by the throat. Am I lying? Yes.
Are you smiling? Yes. I'll follow you, yes? No reply.

To My Father's Business

Leo bends over his desk
Gazing at a memorandum
While Stuart stands beside him
With a smile, saying,
"Leo, the order for those desks
Came in today
From Youngstown Needle and Thread!"
C. Loth Inc., there you are
Like Balboa the conqueror
Of those who want to buy office furniture
Or bar fixtures
In nineteen forty in Cincinnati, Ohio!
Secretaries pound out
Invoices on antique typewriters—
Dactylographs
And fingernail biters.
I am sitting on a desk
Looking at my daddy
Who is proud of but feels unsure about
Some aspects of his little laddie.
I will go on to explore
Deep and/or nonsensical themes
While my father's on the dark hardwood floor
Hit by a couple of Ohio sunbeams.
Kenny, he says, some day you'll work in the store.
But I felt "never more" or "never ever."
Harvard was far away
World War Two was distant
Psychoanalysis was extremely expensive
All of these saved me from you.

C. Loth you made my father happy
I saw his face shining
He laughed a lot, working in you
He said to Miss Ritter
His secretary
"Ritt, this is my boy, Kenny!"
"Hello there Kenny," she said
My heart in an uproar
I loved you but couldn't think
Of staying with you
I can see the virtues now
That could come from being in you
A sense of balance
Compromise and acceptance—
Not isolated moments of brilliance
Like a girl without a shoe,
But someone that you
Care for every day—
Need for customers and the economy
Don't go away.
There were little pamphlets
Distributed in you
About success in business
Each about eight to twelve pages long
One whole series of them
All ended with the words
"P.S. He got the job"
One a story about a boy who said,
"I swept up the street, Sir,
Before you got up." Or
"There were five hundred extra catalogues
So I took them to people in the city who have a dog"—

P.S. He got the job.
I didn't get the job
I didn't think that I could do the job
I thought I might go crazy in the job
Staying in you
You whom I could love
But not be part of.
The secretaries clicked
Their Smith Coronas closed at five p.m.
And took the streetcars to Kentucky then
And I left too.

To Kidding Around

Kidding around you are terrible sometimes
When I feel that I have to do it
Suddenly behaving like an ape, piling up snow on top of
    a friend
When I know that isn't going to win her heart;
Screaming for no reason very loud, eating in a noisy way,
Running and barking as if I were a dog through the
    dimly lighted streets
Frightening the inhabitants, bashing myself into the
    cut-outs
Or mannequins in a store-window display, and yelling
    Boffo!
I am having so much fun
Seemingly. But isn't this a faithless seeming?
For I'm a joker, an ass
And I can't stop being

Ridiculous, my tongue against the window
Vlop vlap I can't get it loose
It's frozen here!
How can I ever say what's in my heart
While imitating the head butts of a rhinoceros
Or the arm spans of an octopus
I am nothing but a wretched clown
All manner
Of humiliating things.
Like a far-off landscape.
Icy women who loom like towers.
Yet sometimes you are breathtaking,
Kidding around!
To be rid of the troubles
Of one person by turning into
Someone else, moving and jolting
As if nothing mattered but today
In fact nothing
But this precise moment—five thirty-one a.m.
Celery growing on the plains
Snow swirls in the mountains.

To World War Two

Early on you introduced me to young women in bars
You were large, and with a large hand
You presented them in different cities,
Made me in San Luis Obispo, drunk
On French seventy-fives, in Los Angeles, on pousse-
    cafés.

It was a time of general confusion
Of being a body hurled at a wall.
I didn't do much fighting. I sat, rather I stood, in a
    foxhole.
I stood while the typhoon splashed us into morning.
It felt unusual
Even if for a good cause
To be part of a destructive force
With my rifle in my hands
And in my head
My serial number
The entire object of my existence
To eliminate Japanese soldiers
By killing them
With a rifle or with a grenade
And then, many years after that,
I could write poetry
Fall in love
And have a daughter
And think
About these things
From a great distance
If I survived
I was "paying my debt
To society" a paid
Killer. It wasn't
Like anything I'd done
Before, on the paved
Streets of Cincinnati
Or on the ballroom floor
At Mr. Vathé's dancing class
What would Anne Marie Goldsmith

Have thought of me
If instead of asking her to dance
I had put my BAR to my shoulder
And shot her in the face
I thought about her in my foxhole—
One, in a foxhole near me, has his throat cut during the
     night
We take more precautions but it is night and it is you.
The typhoon continues and so do you.
"I can't be killed—because of my poetry. I have to live
     on in order to write it."
I thought—even crazier thought, or just as crazy—
"If I'm killed while thinking of lines, it will be too corny
When it's reported" (I imagined it would be reported!)
So I kept thinking of lines of poetry. One that came to
     me on the beach on Leyte
Was "The surf comes in like masochistic lions."
I loved this terrible line. It was keeping me alive. My
     Uncle Leo wrote to me,
 "You won't believe this, but some day you may wish
You were footloose and twenty on Leyte again." I have
     never wanted
To be on Leyte again,
With you, whispering into my ear,
"Go on and win me! Tomorrow you may not be alive,
So do it today!" How could anyone ever win you?
How many persons would I have had to kill
Even to begin to be a part of winning you?
You were too much for me, though I
Was older than you were and in camouflage. But for you
Who threw everything together, and had all the systems

Working for you all the time, this was trivial. If you
        could use me
You'd use me, and then forget. How else
Did I think you'd behave?
I'm glad you ended. I'm glad I didn't die. Or lose my
        mind.
As machines make ice
We made dead enemy soldiers, in
Dark jungle alleys, with weapons in our hands
That produced fire and kept going straight through
I was carrying one,
I who had gone about for years as a child
Praying God don't let there ever be another war
Or if there is, don't let me be in it. Well, I was in you.
All you cared about was existing and being won.
You died of a bomb blast in Nagasaki, and there were
        parades.

To My Twenties

How lucky that I ran into you
When everything was possible
For my legs and arms, and with hope in my heart
And so happy to see any woman—
O woman! O my twentieth year!
Basking in you, you
Oasis from both growing and decay
Fantastic unheard of nine- or ten-year oasis
A palm tree, hey! And then another
And another—and water!

I'm still very impressed by you. Whither,
Midst falling decades, have you gone? Oh in what lucky
    fellow,
Unsure of himself, upset, and unemployable
For the moment in any case, do you live now?
From my window I drop a nickel
By mistake. With
You I race down to get it
But I find there on
The street instead, a good friend,
X—— N——, who says to me
Kenneth do you have a minute?
And I say yes! I am in my twenties!
I have plenty of time! In you I marry,
In you I first go to France; I make my best friends
In you, and a few enemies. I
Write a lot and am living all the time
And thinking about living. I loved to frequent you
After my teens and before my thirties.
You three together in a bar
I always preferred you because you were midmost
Most lustrous apparently strongest
Although now that I look back on you
What part have you played?
You never, ever, were stingy.
What you gave me you gave whole
But as for telling
Me how best to use it
You weren't a genius at that.
Twenties, my soul
Is yours for the asking
You know that, if you ever come back.

To Psychoanalysis

I took the Lexington Avenue subway
To arrive at you in your glory days
Of the Nineteen Fifties when we believed
That you could solve any problem
And I had nothing but disdain
For "self-analysis" "group analysis" "Jungian analysis"
"Adlerian analysis" the Karen Horney kind
All—other than you, pure Freudian type—
Despicable and never to be mine!
I would lie down according to your
Dictates but not go to sleep.
I would free-associate. I would say whatever
Came into my head. Great
Troops of animals floated through
And certain characters like Picasso and Einstein
Whatever came into my head or my heart
Through reading or thinking or talking
Came forward once again in you. I took voyages
Down deep unconscious rivers, fell through fields,
Cleft rocks, went on through hurricanes and volcanoes.
Ruined cities were as nothing to me
In my fantastic advancing. I recovered epochs,
Gold of former ages that melted in my hands
And became toothpaste or hazy vanished citadels. I
     dreamed
Exclusively for you. I was told not to make important
     decisions.
This was perfect. I never wanted to. On the Har-Tru
     surface of my emotions

Your ideas sank in so I could play again.
But something was happening. You gave me an ideal
Of conversation—entirely about me
But including almost everything else in the world.
But this wasn't poetry it was something else.
After two years of spending time in you
Years in which I gave my best thoughts to you
And always felt you infiltrating and invigorating my
      feelings
Two years at five days a week, I had to give you up.
It wasn't my idea. "I think you are nearly through,"
Dr. Loewenstein said. "You seem much better." But,
      Light!
Comedy! Tragedy! Energy! Science! Balance! Breath!
I didn't want to leave you. I cried. I sat up.
I stood up. I lay back down. I sat. I said
But I still get sore throats and have hay fever
"And some day you are going to die. We can't cure
      everything."
Psychoanalysis! I stood up like someone covered with
      light
As with paint, and said Thank you. Thank you.
It was only one moment in a life, my leaving you.
But once I walked out, I could never think of anything
      seriously
For fifteen years without also thinking of you. Now
      what have we become?
You look the same, but now you are a past You.
That's fifties clothing you're wearing. You have some
      fifties ideas
Left—about sex, for example. What shall we do? Go
      walking?

We're liable to have a slightly frumpy look,
But probably no one will notice—another something I
    didn't know then.

To Jewishness

As you were contained in
Or embodied by
Louise Schlossman
When she was a sophomore
At Walnut Hills
High School
In Cincinnati, Ohio,
I salute you
And thank you
For the fact
That she received
My kisses with tolerance
On New Year's Eve
And was not taken aback
As she well might have been
Had she not had you
And had I not, too.
Ah, you!
Dark, complicated you!
Jewishness, you are the tray—
On it painted
Moses, David and the Ten
Commandments, the handwriting

On the Wall, Daniel
In the lions' den—
On which my childhood
Was served
By a mother
And father
Who took you
To Michigan—
Oh the soft smell
Of the pine
Trees of Michigan
And the gentle roar
Of the Lake! Michigan
Or sent you
To Wisconsin—
I went to camp there—
On vacation, with me
Every year!
My counselors had you
My fellow campers
Had you and "Doc
Ehrenreich" who
Ran the camp had you
We got up in the
Mornings you were there
You were in the canoes
And on the baseball
Diamond, everywhere around.
At home, growing
Taller, you
Thrived, too. Louise had you

And Charles had you
And Jean had you
And her sister Mary
Had you
We all had you
And your Bible
Full of stories
That didn't apply
Or didn't seem to apply
In the soft spring air
Or dancing, or sitting in the cars
To anything we did.
In "religious school"
At the Isaac M. Wise
Synagogue (called "temple")
We studied not you
But Judaism, the one who goes with you
And is your guide, supposedly,
Oddly separated
From you, though there
In the same building, you
In us children, and it
On the blackboards
And in the books—Bibles
And books simplified
From the Bible. How
Like a Bible with shoulders
Rabbi Seligmann is!
You kept my parents and me
Out of the hotels near Crystal Lake
In Michigan and you resulted, for me,

In insults,
At which I felt
Chagrined but
Was energized by you.
You went with me
Into the army, where
One night in a foxhole
On Leyte a fellow soldier
Said Where are the fuckin Jews?
Back in the PX. I'd like to
See one of those bastards
Out here. I'd kill him!
I decided to conceal
You, my you, anyway, for a while.
Forgive me for that.
At Harvard you
Landed me in a room
In Kirkland House
With two other students
Who had you. You
Kept me out of the Harvard clubs
And by this time (I
Was twenty-one) I found
I preferred
Kissing girls who didn't
Have you. Blonde
Hair, blue eyes,
And Christianity (oddly enough) had an
Aphrodisiac effect on me.
And everything that opened
Up to me, of poetry, of painting, of music,

Of architecture in old cities
Didn't have you—
I was
Distressed
Though I knew
Those who had you
Had hardly had the chance
To build cathedrals
Write secular epics
(Like *Orlando Furioso*)
Or paint Annunciations—"Well
I had David
In the wings." David
Was a Jew, even a Hebrew.
He wasn't Jewish.
You're quite
Something else. "I had Mahler,
Einstein, and Freud." I didn't
Want those three (then). I wanted
Shelley, Byron, Keats, Shakespeare,
Mozart, Monet. I wanted
Botticelli and Fra Angelico.
"There you've
Chosen some hard ones
For me to connect to. But
Why not admit that I
Gave you the life
Of the mind as a thing
To aspire to? And
Where did you go
To find your 'freedom'? to

New York, which was
Full of me." I do know
Your good qualities, at least
Good things you did
For me—when I was ten
Years old, how you brought
Judaism in, to give ceremony
To everyday things, surprise and
Symbolism and things beyond
Understanding in the
Synagogue then I
Was excited by you, a rescuer
Of me from the flatness of my life.
But then the flatness got you
And I let it keep you
And, perhaps, of all things known,
That was most ignorant. "You
Sound like Yeats, but
You're not. Well, happy
Voyage home, Kenneth, to
The parking lot
Of understood experience. I'll be
Here if you need me and here
After you don't
Need anything else. HERE is a quality
I have, and have had
For you, and for a lot of others,
Just by being it, since you were born."

To the French Language

I needed to find you and, once having found you, to
  keep you
You who could make me a physical Larousse
Of everyday living, you who would present me to Gilberte
And Anna and Sonia, you by whom I could be a surrealist
And a dadaist and almost a fake of Racine and of
  Molière. I was hiding
The heavenly dolor you planted in my heart:
That I would never completely have you.
I wanted to take you with me on long vacations
Always giving you so many kisses, ma française—
Across rocky mountains, valleys, and lakes
And I wanted it to be as if
Nous faisions ce voyage pour l'éternité
Et non pas uniquement pour la brève durée d'une année
  boursière en France.
Those days, and that idea, are gone.
A little hotel on the rue de Fleurus
Was bursting with you.
And one April morning, when I woke up, I had you
Stuck to the tip of my tongue like a Christmas sticker
I walked out into the street, it was Fleurus
And said hello which came out Bonjour Madame
I walked to the crémerie four doors away and sat down.
I was lifted up by you. I knew I couldn't be anything to
  you
But an aspiring lover. Sans ego. It was the best
  relationship
Of relationships sans ego, that I've ever had.

I know you love flattery and are so good at it that one
    can hardly believe
What you are saying when it is expressed in you.
But I have loved you. That's no flattering statement
But the truth. And still love you, though now I'm not in
    love with you.
The woman who first said this to me nearly broke my
    heart,
But I don't think I'm breaking yours, because it's a coeur
In the first place and, for another thing, it beats under le
    soleil
On a jeudi or vendredi matin and besides you're not
    listening to me
At least not as you did on the days
I sat around in Aix-en-Provence's cafés waiting for you
To spark a conversation—about nothing in particular. I
    was on stage
At all times, and you were the script and the audience
Even when the theatre had no people in it, you were
    there.

To Old Age

You hurried through my twenties as if there were
    nowhere to look
For what you were searching for, perhaps my first trip to
    China.
You said, "I love that country because they love every-
    thing that's old

And they like things to look old—take the fortune
    cookies for example
Or the dumplings or the universe's shining face." I said,
"Chopsticks don't look old," but you were hurrying
Past me, past my love, my uncomprehended marriage, my
Nine or ten years nailed in the valley of the fools, and
    still you were not there,
Wouldn't stop there. You disappeared for a year
That I spent in Paris, carne back to me in my father's face
And later in my mother's conversation. You seemed
    great in the palm trees
During a storm and lessened by the boats' preceding
    clops.
Looking at a gun or at a tiger I never thought I was
    standing facing you.
You were elsewhere, rippling the sands or else making
    some boring conversation
Among people who scarcely knew each other. You were
    left by Shelley to languish
And by Byron and by Keats. Shakespeare never encoun-
    tered you. What are you, old age,
That some do and some do not come to you?
Are you an old guru who won't quit talking to us in time
For us to hang up the phone? You scare me half to death
And I suppose you will take me there, too. You are a
    companion
Of green ivy and stumbling vines. If I could break away
    from you
I would, but there is no light down in that gulch there.
    Walk with me, then
Let's not be falling . . . this fiery morning. *Grand âge,
nous voici!* Old age, here we are!

Mountain

Nothing's moving I don't see anybody
And I know that it's not a trick
There really is nothing moving there
And there aren't any people. It is the very utmost top
Where, as is not unusual,
There is snow, lying like the hair on a white-haired
      person's head
Combed sideways and backward and forward to cover as
      much of the top
As possible, for the snow is thinning, it's September
Although a few months from now there will be a new
      crop
Probably, though this no one KNOWS (so neither do we)
But every other year it has happened by November
Except for one year that's known about, nineteen
      twenty-three
When the top was more and more uncovered until
      December fifteenth
When finally it snowed and snowed
I love seeing this mountain like a mouse
Attached to the tail of another mouse, and to another
      and to another
In total mountain silence
There is no way to get up there, and no means to stay.
It is uninhabitable. No roads and no possibility
Of roads. You don't have a history
Do you, mountain top? This doesn't make you either a
      mystery
Or a dull person and you're certainly not a truck stop.

No industry can exploit you
No developer can divide you into estates or lots
No dazzling disquieting woman can tie your heart in
knots.
I could never lead my life on one of those spots
You leave uncovered up there. No way to be there
But I'm moved.

Proverb

Les morts vont vite, the dead go fast, the next day absent!
Et les vivants sont dingues, the living are haywire.
Except for a few who grieve, life rapidly readjusts itself
The milliner trims the hat not thinking of the departed
The horse sweats and throws his stubborn rider to the
earth
Uncaring if he has killed him or not
The thrown man rises. But now he knows that he is not
going,
Not going fast, though he was close to having been gone.
The day after Caesar's death, there was a new, bustling
Rome
The moment after the racehorse's death, a new one is
sought for the stable
The second after a moth's death there are one or two
hundred other moths
The month after Einstein's death the earth is inundated
with new theories
Biographies are written to cover up the speed with
which we go:

No more presence in the bedroom or waiting in the hall
Greeting to say hello with mixed emotions. The dead go
    quickly
Not knowing why they go or where they go. To die is
    human,
To come back divine. Roosevelt gives way to Truman
Suddenly in the empty White House a brave new voice
    resounds
And the wheelchaired captain has crossed the great
    divide.
Faster than memories, faster than old mythologies,
    faster than the speediest train.
Alexander of Macedon, on time!
Prudhomme on time, Gorbachev on time, the beloved
    and the lover on time!
Les morts vont vite. We living stand at the gate
And life goes on.

At Extremes

I had a dream about a polar bear
He seemed to want to inform me about something.
I have had a psychoanalyst but I have never had a
    soothsayer.
Even if my soothsayer were a polar bear I would not
    believe her (or him).
The men I see giving speeches in the public square
    know nothing at all
About anything I care about except how to move crowds

They like to move crowds the way Shelley wanted the
    West Wind to move his product.
Each might go and live with Janice in Florence in nine-
    teen fifty-four.
Each might wake up some early spring morning oddly
    wishing to eat a piece of hard candy.
A former student of mine is doing very well, I hear, but
    his chronic anxiety
Makes him dissatisfied and unhappy, fearful that people
    don't appreciate him.
Well, some people appreciate him but he isn't satisfied
    with that.
He is sufficiently intelligent and ambitious but he gets
    headaches.
He will not go to Florence to live with Janice in 1954.
I am the only person in the whole history of the world
    ever to have done that.
No one knows when he or she is going to die. The polar
    bear probably never thinks about it.
He is wholly committed to life, unlike my former student,
Unlike Janice, unlike me. We are all committed to the
    life product.
What power is there in having done something once and
    then knowing automatically that it is for all time!
One, wearing a bathing costume of white featuring red
    dots, politely smiles,
If you don't try to come on to me I will show you the cliff
At which dolphins jump, but I couldn't promise
I used to say you don't need the sun when you travel first
    class
We were living in Greece unswayed by politicians

But we could be mightily moved by changes in the
    economy
Janice said to me one very hot summer day look at my
    feet
I said they're nice She said I didn't mean that, you silly
I mean look at all the tar on them from being on this
    beach
At that time there were no houses close to the sea.
You have to go back to your house.
You sleep there. Hotels are invented.
A hotel is where when you go there they have to let you in
If a room is available and you can convince them you
    can pay.
Michelangelo leaves Florence. He is just a man.
Ruskin and Michelangelo face each other across an
    oaken table.
When you are free it is hard to decide what is best.
There are no rooms in the hotel.
But now there is one. It hasn't been swept recently.
There is dust on the floor.
Gratefully, Michelangelo Antonioni sinks into a deep
    slumber.
Four of his great films are already made and another one
    is to follow.
The sheep were the best men at the sheepflies' wedding.
A noun perturbs an adjective with its slightly superior
    social class.
I'm the thing itself, the noun says.
Stay in love said Michelangelo and Antonioni woke up.
    Being bareheaded was serious business
In an arctic wind.

We were in good physical condition and not depressed.
We were fifty percent men and fifty percent women
We were afraid that half of us might be squid.
The nouns, wishing to be pampered, call the adjectives
     back
But it is the verbs, here by this thundering surf, that are
     triumphant.
Octopuses come bearing blue-hatted children on their
     backs.
In a hotel you may sometimes find geniuses around
Probably they won't speak to you unless they need
     company.
Children clamber up to the roof of the hotel
Silently one of them wishes he or she were an octopus
Then one would be one's own village maybe one's own
     city
How could I have need, a child thinks, for anyone then?
The bird flies over the gray, deserted porch of the hotel.
I am the only one who saw Miss X at four-fifteen in the
     afternoon on June 2nd for the first time while
     attempting in a slight fit of nervousness to light
     up a Camel.
You are difficult to smuggle through customs.
Gypsy romance makes its appearance.
Everyone was fairly well satisfied—or almost—with
     someone else,
Even the ones who listen to the speakers and the one
     who walks around the city with his hands behind his
     back.
In Vinalhaven the old-timer's baseball game proceeds—
For some people, "reality" is represented by a prostitute,
     just plain business. Get down to facts.

The facts are that when you are fourteen or fifteen you
   want sex.
In some way or another you are going to get it.
By what process this turns into something with
   dominion over your life is unknown.
Theories abound. Small-town railroad stations. Bus
   stops. Inventions to replace teeth by glass.
Winter is ignorance. She picks the rose apart, trembling,
   with life in her fingers.
The polar bear swims toward the dam. He is part of a
   continuum.

Paradiso

There is no way not to be excited
When what you have been disillusioned by raises its
   head
From its arms and seems to want to talk to you again.
You forget home and family
And set off on foot or in your automobile
And go to where you believe this form of reality
May dwell. Not finding it there, you refuse
Any further contact
Until you are back again trying to forget
The only thing that moved you (it seems) and gave what
   you forever will have
But in the form of a disillusion.
Yet often, looking toward the horizon
There—inimical to you?—is that something you have
   never found

And that, without those who came before you, you could
    never have imagined.
How could you have thought there was one person who
    could make you
Happy and that happiness was not the uneven
Phenomenon you have known it to be? Why do you
    keep believing in this
Reality so dependent on the time allowed it
That it has less to do with your exile from the age you
    are
Than from everything else life promised that you
    could do?

BIOGRAPHICAL NOTE

Kenneth Koch was born on February 25, 1927, in Cincinnati, Ohio. He attended the University of Cincinnati until he was drafted into the U.S. Army, where he served as an infantryman during World War II and fought in the Pacific at the battle of Leyte and elsewhere. After his discharge in 1946 he enrolled at Harvard, where he studied with Delmore Schwartz and edited the *Harvard Advocate*. He moved to New York and pursued graduate studies at Columbia, which was punctuated by a year spent in France as a Fulbright fellow (1951–52). His first volume, the chapbook *Poems*, was published in 1953. Koch was a prolific writer of poems, plays, and fiction, whose books include *One Thousand Avant-Garde Plays* (1988) and *On the Great Atlantic Rainway: Selected Poems 1950–1988* (1994). For more than four decades a professor at Columbia, he was also known for conducting writing workshops, including those for children and the elderly. He died of leukemia in New York City on July 6, 2002.

NOTE ON THE TEXTS

The texts of the poems in this volume are taken from Koch's *Collected Poems* (New York: Knopf, 2005). In one poem, "A Time Zone," the present volume restores a passage inadvertently omitted from the first printing of *Collected Poems* (from "Frank's visiting" [126.19] to ". . . like a pear" [129.28]).

The poems in this volume were included in the following individual volumes of Koch's poetry:

Sun Out: *Sun Out: Selected Poems 1952–54* (New York: Knopf, 2000)

To You; The Circus ("We will have to go away, said the girls in the circus"); Permanently; You Were Wearing; Variations on a Theme by William Carlos Williams; The Railway Stationery; Fresh Air: *Thank You and Other Poems* (New York: Grove, 1962).

The Pleasures of Peace: *The Pleasures of Peace* (New York: Grove, 1969).

The Circus ("I remember when I wrote The Circus"); Alive for an Instant; Some General Instructions; The Art of Poetry: *The Art of Love* (New York: Random House, 1975).

The Boiling Water; To Marina: *The Burning Mystery of Anna in 1951* (New York: Random House, 1979).

Days and Nights: *Days and Nights* (New York: Random House, 1982)

One Train May Hide Another; A Time Zone: *One Train* (New York: Knopf, 1994)

Straits; Currency; from Songs from the Plays: *Straits* (New York: Knopf, 1998)

To "Yes"; To My Father's Business; To Kidding Around; To World War Two;

To My Twenties; To Psychoanalysis; To Jewishness; To the French Language; To Old Age: *New Addresses* (New York: Knopf, 2000)

Mountain; Proverb; At Extremes; Paradiso: *A Possible World* (New York: Knopf, 2002)

In addition to the restored passage cited above, the present volume has emended the text of the 2005 Knopf edition of *Collected Poems* in four instances: 21.12, fahrenheit; 26.28, test"; 122.26, *Ladies*; 175.17, Octopus.

ACKNOWLEDGMENTS

One might think that it would be difficult for three people to agree quickly on a selection of the best and most representative pieces from the approximately 750 published pages of Kenneth Koch's shorter poems, but when Karen Koch, Jordan Davis, and I—the executors of the Kenneth Koch Literary Estate— were called upon to make a selection, we were pleasantly surprised by how many of our choices were identical. That it was not coincidental was confirmed by the recommendations made to us by David Lehman, who originated the idea of this volume.

Many thanks to Katherine Koch for information about and insights into her father. She provided a helpful critique of a draft of this book's introduction, as did Bill Berkson, Jane Freilicher, and my wife, Patricia. I have also benefited greatly from conversations over the years with Michael Anania, John Ashbery, Paul Auster, Bill Berkson, Ted Berrigan, Jim Dine, Bertrand Dorny, Kenward Elmslie, Larry Fagin, Kate Farrell, Dick Gallup, Emily and Dermot Harvey, Siri Hustvedt, Jim Jarmusch, Alex Katz, Ann Lauterbach, Joe LeSueur, Harry Mathews, Charles North, Alice Notley, Anne Porter, Larry Rivers, George Schneeman, James Schuyler, David Shapiro,

Mark Statman, Lorenzo Thomas, Tony Towle, Paul Violi, Anne Waldman, Anne Walker, and Bill Zavatsky. Shapiro is a walking anthology of quotations from Kenneth's conversation.

Invaluable was the help I received from Stephen Crook, Philip Milito, and Nina Schneider, who deftly located papers in the Kenneth Koch Archive at the New York Public Library's Berg Collection, curated by Dr. Isaac Gewirtz. I am also grateful to Dr. Ernest True of Norwich University, who provided information on the Pacific campaign of World War Two, and to the Kellogg-Hubbard Library of Montpelier, Vermont.

Readers whose appetite for Koch's poetry is whetted by this volume have several dazzling banquets awaiting them in the form of his *Collected Poems* and *Collected Long Poems*, both published by Ann Close of Alfred A. Knopf, who have generously allowed us to use material from the former volume. Also not to be missed are Koch's *Collected Fiction*, his plays, comics, anthologies, and books about reading and writing poetry.

It is a blessing to work closely with smart, good-natured, tireless people. Karen and Jordan, thank you.

Ron Padgett

INDEX OF TITLES
AND FIRST LINES

AMERICAN POETS PROJECT